The Grammar School, Stratford on Avon

THE
ALDUS
SHAKESPEARE

WITH COPIOUS NOTES AND COMMENTS BY
HENRY NORMAN HUDSON, M.A.,
ISRAEL GOLLANCZ, M.A.,
C. H. HERFORD, LITT. D.,
AND OVER ONE HUNDRED OTHER
EMINENT SHAKESPEAREAN AUTHORITIES.

COMEDY
OF
ERRORS

BIGELOW SMITH & CO.
NEW YORK

THE COMEDY OF ERRORS

All the unsigned footnotes in this volume are by the writer of the article to which they are appended. The interpretation of the initials signed to the others is: I. G. = Israel Gollancz, M.A.; H. N. H.= Henry Norman Hudson, A.M.; C. H. H.= C. H. Herford, Litt.D.

PREFACE

By Israel Gollancz, M.A.

THE FIRST EDITION

The Comedy of Errors first appeared in the Folio of 1623, where it immediately follows *Measure for Measure*. "The names of all the actors" are not given at the end of the play as in the case of the previous plays; in the stage-directions to the first two Acts the two *Antipholi* are distinguished as *Antipholus Erotes* and *Antipholus Sereptus;* the latter title was probably derived from the *Menæchmus Surreptus* of Plautus, a character evidently well-known to the Elizabethans (*cp.* Cambridge Shakespeare, Note 1); as regards the former name, it is noteworthy that *Erotion* (also *Errotis* in Act II.) is the name of "the Courtezan" in Plautus' *Menæchmi;* to this source the name may perhaps be referred; otherwise it must be regarded as an error for *Erraticus* or *Errans*.

The Comedy of Errors is the shortest of all Shakespeare's plays; its total number of lines is 1,770.

DATE OF COMPOSITION

The Comedy of Errors is mentioned in 1598 by Meres in his *Palladis Tamia* among the six "excellent" comedies of Shakespeare. In the *Gesta Grayorum* of 1594 occurs what is probably the earliest reference to the play:—

"After such sport, a Comedy of Errors (like to Plautus his Menechmus) was played by the players; so that night began and continued to the end, in nothing but confusion and errors; whereupon it was ever afterwards called the Night of Errors." There are other references to comedies

vii

of "Errors" (a *Historie of Error* was acted by the St.
Paul's children at Greenwich as early as New Year 1576–7),
but they merely indicate that the phrase was proverbial.
Certain critics detect in these pre-Shakespearean plays the
original of Shakespeare's Comedy.

One or two points of internal evidence are helpful in fixing the approximate time of composition. In Act III. ii.
125 there is evidently an allusion to the civil war in France
between Henry III and Henry of Navarre, which lasted
from August, 1589, to July, 1593. Further, the reference to "whole armadoes of caracks" in the same scene
suggests the earlier rather than the later limit: the play
may safely be dated 1589–91.[1] This early date is corro-
borated by the general style of the play:—its lyrical passages with rhyming couplets and alternate rhymes; the
doggerel verse; the abundance of quibbles and word-play;
"the prologue-like" speech of Ægeon in the opening
scene; lines suggestive of other early plays (*e.g.* Act II. ii.
201, reminds us of *Midsummer-Night's Dream; cp.* Act IV.
i. 93, and *Love's Labor's Lost*, II. i. 219, and *Two Gentlemen of Verona*, I. i. 72).

SOURCES OF THE PLOT

The main plot of *The Comedy of Errors* is directly or
indirectly derived from the *Menæchmi* of Plautus,—"a
farce of mistaken identity," which very early in the history of the modern drama became a favorite theme with
dramatists: pre-Shakespearean paraphrases and adaptations
exist in French, German, and Italian; the interlude of
"*Jack Juggler*" (1563) is probably its earliest representa-
tive in English literature. The oldest extant English
translation appeared in the year 1595, with the following
title:—*Menæcmi, A pleasant and fine conceited Comedie,
taken out of the most excellent wittie Poet Plautus.
Chosen purposely from out the rest, as least harmefull,*

[1] *Cp. An attempt to determine Chronological Order of Shakespeare's Plays;* H. P. Stokes, pp. 16–20.

and yet most delightfull. Written in English, by W. W. (i.e. *"William Warner"*). . . . 1595. The translation is in prose; an argument in verse precedes:—

> "Two Twinborn sons, a Sicill merchant had,
> Menechmus one, and Soseles the other:
> The first his Father lost, a little lad,
> The Grandsire named the latter like his brother.
> This (grown a man) long travel took to seek
> His brother, and to Epidamnum came,
> Where th' other dwelt inriched, and him so like,
> That Citizens there take him for the same:
> Father, wife, neighbours, each mistaking either,
> *Much pleasant error,* ere they meet togither."

These lines may serve to indicate the leading points of difference between the simple Latin farce and the complex *Comedy of Errors*. (The translation is to be found in Hazlitt's *Shakespeare's Library*, Part II. vol. 1.)

It is impossible to determine whether Shakespeare owes anything to Warner's translation, which may have existed in manuscript long before the date of its entry on the books of the Stationers' Company (1594). It is perhaps noteworthy that Adriana in the *Comedy* and the wife of Menechus the Citizen in the English translation both use the same word with reference to their supposed ignoble treatment:—

Senex. What is the matter?
Mulier. He makes me a stale and a laughing-stock to all the world.

cp. *Comedy of Errors*, Act. II. i. 100:—

Adriana. He breaks the pale,
And feeds from home; poor I am but his stale.

A few minor points of this description (*e.g.* the use of "error" in the last line of the Argument) have led some scholars to the conclusion that Shakespeare had read Warner's version of the play. But may not the translator owe this small debt to the dramatist?

Act III. Scene i. seems to have been derived from the

Amphitruo of Plautus; in the Latin comedy Mercury keeps the real Amphitruo out of his own house, while Jupiter, the sham Amphitruo, is within with Alcmena, the real Amphitruo's wife.

The introduction of the twin Dromios is Shakespeare's own device; and all the pathos of the play is his; there is nothing in the Latin original suggestive of Ægeon's touching story at the opening of the play,—in Plautus, the father of the twins is already dead. and there is no reunion of husband, wife, and children.

THE UNITIES

In spite, however, of this romanticizing of Plautus, Shakespeare has maintained throughout the play the hallowed unities of time and place, "the necessary companions," according to Academic criticism, "of all corporal actions." From this point of view *The Comedy of Errors* may be regarded as the final triumph of the New Romantic Drama over its opponents; it carried the warfare into the enemy's camp, and scored the signal victory of harmonizing Old and New,—the conventional canons of Latin Comedy and the pathos of Romanticism.

INTRODUCTION

By Henry Norman Hudson, A.M.

The Comedy of Errors bears upon its face indubitable marks of being one of Shakespeare's earliest performances. In respect to merit, most readers, we apprehend, would be apt to place it at the bottom of the list of comedies; though this may be owing more to the nature of the subject than to the manner of the execution. It was mentioned by Meres in 1598; which was supposed to be the earliest notice of it extant, until very lately Mr. Halliwell brought to light a passage in the *Gesta Grayorum*, showing that it was acted at Gray's Inn during the Christmas revels in 1594. The writer concludes his account of one day's proceedings thus: "After such sports, a Comedy of Errors, like to Plautus his Menechmus, was played by the players: so that night was begun and continued to the end in nothing but confusion and errors, whereupon it was ever afterwards called the 'Night of Errors.'" Mr. Halliwell also shows that the title was either a common proverb or furnished the subject of one. But one other contemporary notice of the play has been produced, and that is from the account of the Master of the Revels, showing it to have been acted at Whitehall, December 28, 1604: "By his Majesty's players: On Innocents' Night, the play of Errors." And "Shaxberd" is written in the margin as "the name of the poet which made the play." The play itself, however, has one passage that may go somewhat to ascertain its date. It is in Act iii. sc. 2, where Dromio of Syracuse, talking of the "kitchen wench," who made love to him, and who was "spherical like a globe," so that he "could find out countries in her," in answer to the question,—"Where France?" says,—"In her forehead; arm'd and reverted, making war against her heir." Which was probably meant for a quibble between heir and hair, and referred to the civil war that broke out in France in 1589, upon the death of Henry III; otherwise there were no apparent point in the jest. As this war against the heir of France was because of his being a Protestant, the English people took great interest in it; so that the allusion would naturally be understood and relished: and it agrees entirely with what appears on other grounds to have been the date of the play.—*The Comedy of Errors* was not printed nor entered in the Stationers' books till the folio of 1623, where it makes the fifth in the division of Comedies.

There has been considerable speculation and quite a variety of opinions as to whether Shakespeare wrote the whole of this play—a matter that need not be better stated than it has been by Mr. Singer. "The general idea of this play," says he, "is taken from the *Menæchmi* of Plautus, but the plot is entirely recast and rendered much more diverting by the variety and quick succession of the incidents. To the twin brothers of Plautus are added twin servants, and though this increases the improbability, yet, as Schlegel observes, 'when once we have lent ourselves to the first, which certainly borders on the incredible, we should not probably be disposed to cavil about the second; and if the spectator is to be entertained with mere perplexities, they cannot be too much varied.' The clumsy and inartificial mode of informing the spectator by a prologue of events, which it was necessary for him to be acquainted with in order to enter into the spirit of the piece, is well avoided, and shows the superior skill of the modern dramatist over his ancient prototype. With how much more propriety is it placed in the mouth of Ægeon, the father of the twin brothers, whose character is sketched with such skill as deeply to interest the reader in his griefs and misfortunes. Development of character, however, was not to be expected in a piece which consists of an uninter-

upted series of mistakes and laughter-moving situations.
Steevens most resolutely maintains his opinion that this
was a play only retouched by the hand of Shakespeare, but
he has not given the grounds upon which his opinion was
formed. We may suppose the doggerel verses of the
drama and the want of distinct characterization in the
Dramatis Personæ, together with the farcelike nature of
some of the incidents, made him draw this conclusion. Ma-
lone has given a satisfactory answer to the first objection,
by adducing numerous examples of the same kind of long
verse from the dramas of several of his contemporaries;
and that Shakespeare was swayed by custom in introducing
it into his early plays there can be no doubt; for it should
be remembered that this kind of versification is to be found
in *Love's Labor's Lost*, and in *The Taming of the Shrew*.
His better judgment made him subsequently abandon it.
. . . It is difficult to pronounce decidedly between the
conflicting opinions of the critics, but the general impression upon my mind is that the whole of the play is
from the hand of Shakespeare. Dr. Drake thinks it 'is
visible throughout the entire play, as well in the broad ex-
uberance of its mirth, as in the cast of its more chastized
parts, a combination of which may be found in the character of Pinch, who is sketched in his strongest and most
marked style.' We may conclude with Schlegel, that 'this
is the best of all written or possible *Menæchmi;* and if the
piece be inferior in worth to other pieces of Shakespeare,
it is merely because nothing more could be made of the ma-
terials.' "

A like diversity of opinions has arisen concerning the immediate sources of the plot of this play. Mr. Collier has
found out that an old drama, entitled *The History of Error,* had been acted at Hampton Court, January 1, 1577,
and probably again at Windsor, on Twelfth night, 1583.
This he conjectures to have been taken as the basis of
Shakespeare's comedy, and that parts of it, especially the
doggerel verses, were interwoven with the Poet's work.
The older play not having been recovered, nor any part of

it, of course we have no means either of refuting or of verifying this conjecture. We may remark, however, that Mr. Collier seems a little too prone to suspect Shakespeare to have borrowed all his puerilities.—Another opinion supposes the Poet to have drawn from a free version of the *Menæchmi* published in 1595, as "A pleasant and fine conceited Comedy, taken out of the most excellent witty Poet Plautus." This version, to be sure, did not come out till after *The Comedy of Errors* was written; but then Shakespeare may have seen it in manuscript; for in his preface the translator speaks of having "divers of this poet's comedies Englished, for the use and delight of his private friends, who in Plautus' own words are not able to understand them." Nevertheless, we are far from thinking such to have been the case; there being no such verbal or other resemblances between the two, as, had such been the case, could scarce have been avoided. The accurate Ritson has ascertained that of this version not a single peculiar name, or phrase, or thought, is to be traced in Shakespeare's comedy. On the whole, we cannot discover the slightest objection to supposing, along with Knight and Verplanck, that the Poet may have drawn directly from Plautus himself; the matter common to them both not being such but that it may well enough have been taken by one who had "small Latin."

The Comedy of Errors is thus disposed of by Coleridge: "Shakespeare has in this piece presented us with a legitimate farce in exactest consonance with the philosophical principles and character of farce, as distinguished from comedy and from entertainments. A proper farce is mainly distinguished from comedy by the license allowed, and even required, in the fable, in order to produce strange and laughable situations. The story need not be probable, it is enough that it be possible. A comedy would scarcely allow even the two Antipholuses; because, although there have been instances of almost indistinguishable likeness in two persons, yet these are mere individual accidents, *casus ludentis naturæ*, and the *verum* will not excuse the *inveri-*

simile. But farce dares add the two Dromios, and is justified in so doing by the laws of its end and constitution. In a word, farces commence in a postulate, which must be granted."

COMMENTS

By SHAKESPEAREAN SCHOLARS

THE PURPOSE OF THE PLAY

The comedy appears to be an amusing satire on man's power of observation and recognition. The accidental resemblance of two pairs of twins, suffices to put almost a whole town into confusion. Life, itself, is conceived, so to say, as a great and many-jointed mistake, encountered by ignorance and blunders in all possible forms. Hence at the very outset we find the life of the father of the two twin brothers in danger, owing to an ignorance of the Ephesian law—a secondary motive of the action which might otherwise appear a mere superfluous appendage. Hence Adriana's unreasonable jealousy of her husband, which again is but a mistake and gives rise to further mistakes. Hence the perpetually increasing complication, which in time deprives all the dramatic characters of their proper consciousness, and which accordingly is not solved till the two pairs of twins stand face to face, although the possibility of two such pairs of twins being confounded is sufficiently obvious. Under the cloak of the comic we have striking evidence of the, in reality, very serious experience in life, that human knowledge and ignorance dovetail into one another and are mixed up together; that it is very easy for that which we suppose ourselves to know most surely and most distinctly, to turn out erroneous and delusive. The wife mistakes her husband, the master his servant, and the servant his master, the sister-in-law her brother-in-law, the friend his friend, and finally even the father his son. In this way the simplest, most natural and most important fundamental relations of life become a chaotic complication and dispute. We are shown how quickly everything becomes confused and perverted, as soon as one of the laws of life—a perfectly external and apparently unimportant law—is broken by a freak of nature, as soon as but the difference of the outward form—by means of which the perception of the senses distinguishes one individual from another—is destroyed. The psychological improbability, spoken of above, is introduced into this general confusion and complication like an integral part of the whole. I mean to say that the fact of Antipholus of Syracuse being bewildered by the strange things that befall him—his forgetting his own intention, his losing sight of the aim and object of his journey and overlooking just that with which he himself stands in obvious relation—agrees perfectly with the meaning of the play, as well as with the bold and strongly-marked outlines in which the young poet has sketched his picture.—ULRICI, *Shakspeare's Dramatic Art*.

ÆGEON

Still more significant is, finally, the story of Ægeon, which envelops the whole comic plot. It is probably Shakespeare's invention, and betrays the same instinct for accumulated effects and drastic contrasts. He had quadrupled the intricacies of the imbroglio by doubling the two lost Antipholuses with a second pair of twins; he quadruples the excitement of the final recovery by doubling them with a pair of lost parents, who at the same time recover their children and each other. And the foreboding of tragic harms which habitually overhangs for a while the early comedies, is here graver and more protracted than either in *A Midsummer-Night's Dream* or *The Two Gentlemen*. Valentine's banishment and Hermia's destination to a nunnery or death arouse no serious suspense; but Ægeon is a pathetic and moving figure, whose story—a masterpiece of Shakespeare's early narrative—strikes a note at the outset with which the subsequent action is in

somewhat too marked dissonance for ripe art.—HERFORD,
The Eversley Shakespeare.

ADRIANA

Shakespeare has depicted jealousy both from its tragic
as well as from its comic side, in "Othello," in "The Winter's Tale," and in "The Merry Wives;" but nowhere in
his works has he portrayed a jealous woman, except
Adriana in "The Comedy of Errors," ii. 1, and v. 1, who
gets the worst of it. Is this accident, or may it not rather
intimate that, according to the ideas of the time, jealousy
was justified in the man, but not in the woman?—ELZE,
William Shakespeare.

The penance for marrying a fortune, in forfeiture of
conjugal subordination and the independence dear to man,
is a frequent theme and evidently founded on conjugal
facts in ancient society;—for aught I know the facts may
be the same in modern. At any rate the modern play
makes excellent use of the hint; Adriana, like the wife of
Menæchmus, brought a wealthy dowry to her husband,
and with it the complementary temper of excessive require-
ments—

> My wife is shrewish when I keep not hours.

At her first appearance she is fretful and peevish at his
want of punctuality, and suspicious of the cause, which,
in truth, as presently appears, was nothing more than a
service and attention intended for herself—"to see the
making of a carcanet," designed as a present for her. Her
husband, on the other hand, enraged at being so inex-
plicably shut out of his own house, disregards the sober
counsel of Balthazar, and is as little practised as his wife
to assume a reason and wait for an explanation, and has-
tily revenges himself by making a bachelor's party at the
house of the courtezan; and though the extravagance is
evidently as harmless as such an imprudence might be; for,

> I know a wench of excellent discourse,
> Pretty and witty, wild, and yet too, gentle,

are not the words of a sensualist, and there is no trace
whatever of want of affection on his part, and we give full
belief to his protestation, he still puts himself by the imprudence no less in the wrong than his wife by her fret-
fulness, and we are left at liberty to enjoy the fun that
arises out of their troubles and disasters. Still Adriana,
with all her shrewishness, is very affectionate—nay, very
amiable, and she gives an earnest of her future improve-
ment in considerateness, by abstaining from public out-
break against her husband's hostess. Her coolness in this
respect requires perhaps more explanation than it receives,
but that it is accepted by us as at once proof and admission
that she had no serious ground for complaint, and was
conscious how far she had herself to blame.—LLOYD, *Critical Essays.*

The wife herself and her sister are studied with a care
and minuteness which the action certainly did not require.
In the change from Plautus' "Mulier," who rails at her
husband with only too good reason, to Shakespeare's
Adriana, who torments him with doubts at bed and board,
and is ready to die in despair at the loss of his love because he refuses to come home to dinner, we see the change
from pragmatical to psychological drama, from the comedy of intrigue to the comedy of character, of which otherwise there is not in this play very much. And Luciana
brings us altogether into the atmosphere of lyric love which
pervades *The Two Gentlemen* and the greater part of *A
Midsummer-Night's Dream*, and is half seriously dispar-
aged in *Love's Labor's Lost.*—HERFORD, *The Eversley
Shakespeare.*

When we read Adriana's speeches, we cannot wonder that
Antipholus of Ephesus, a pleasure-loving young gentleman, as we see later on, often seeks his pleasure away from
home. Such a woman, be she ever so fair and charming,

is not fitted to chain a man to the domestic hearth. On the contrary, she turns his home into a hell by her cross and peevish jealousy, which he avoids as often and as long as he can, seeking outside the peace and quiet his wife will not permit him to enjoy.—LEWES, *The Women of Shakespeare*.

PINCH

Pinch the conjuror is also an excrescence not to be found in Plautus. He is indeed a very formidable anachronism.

> "They brought one Pinch, a hungry lean-fac'd villain,
> A mere anatomy, a mountebank,
> A thread-bare juggler and a fortune-teller;
> A needy, holy-ey'd, sharp-looking wretch,
> A living dead man."

This is exactly like some of the Puritanical portraits to be met with in Hogarth.—HAZLITT, *Characters of Shakespeare's Play*.

SIMILARITY TO THE COMEDIES OF THE ANCIENTS

The color of the old Roman drama is still strongly reflected upon the double twins—they are such masters and such slaves as we are familiar with in the comedy of the ancients, Greek as well as Latin; and, notwithstanding the indications of Christian date, the Abbess and her priory, Pentecost, the protestation on the faith of a Christian, and so forth, the imagination attires them, and requires that they should be attired in representation, in the more uniform costume of classical times, that best lends itself to the misapprehension of identity. The same remark applies to Ægeon, and perhaps Solinus the Duke, yet not so absolutely. Angelo and Balthazar, on the other hand, and also Adriana and her sister, are of true Italian parentage, and might be encountered on the Rialto at Venice at any time, or in the shadows of Palladian architecture at Padua, and should be dressed accordingly; and lastly, Pinch, as English in all his properties as in name, might fitly walk abroad in the gown of any pedagogue of the old free grammar-school at Stratford-upon-Avon. Correct chronology and geography are matters on which no part of the effect of the play would depend, and the obligation of observing them is renounced once for all by divarications of which the decidedness and the consciousness are not to be mistaken; and it would be a great mistake to endeavor to obliterate in the costume presented to the eye, the incongruities which Shakespeare not merely allowed to strike the ear, but actually incorporated with the very structure of his piece, marking them with a degree of distinctness which declares them intentional, and forbids the pedantry that would refine them away into archæological exactitudes, or fall back on an apology for them as oversights.—LLOYD, *Critical Essays*.

The Comedy of Errors, a comedy of incident, of almost farcical adventure [is] the sole attempt of Shakespeare at imitation of the comic drama of ancient Rome. In this play Shakespeare gaily confronts improbabilities, and requires the spectator to accept them. He adds to the twins Antipholus the twins Dromio. If we are in for improbability, let us at least be repaid for it by fun, and have that in abundance. Let the incredible become a twofold incredibility, and it is none the worse. We may conclude that, while Shakespeare was ready to try his hand upon a farcical subject, a single experiment satisfied him that this was not his province; for to such subjects he never returned.— DOWDEN, *Shakspere—His Mind and Art*.

A FARCE

The Comedy of Errors is Shakspere's one farcical play. Its sources of laughter lie almost wholly in the situations and incidents, hardly at all in the characters. The spectator of the play is called on to accept much that is improbable and all but impossible, not as in *A Midsummer Night's Dream*, for the sake of freer play of imagination, and because the world pictured by the poet is a fairy-world of romantic beauty and grotesqueness, but for the sake of mere fun and laughter-stirring surprises. So cleverly, however, are the incidents and persons entangled and disentangled, so rapidly does surprise follow surprise, that we are given no time to raise difficulties and offer objections.—DOWDEN, *Shakespere* in the *Literature Primers*.

Indeed, *The Comedy of Errors* may be pronounced as Shakespeare's only Farce. A perfect Farce, like a perfect Comedy, requires no scenic effect, or change of scene. But unlike comedy, which deals with life and with the verities, and whose characters must be always true, Farce requires that exaggeration at the expense of truth which shall produce only comic situation and cater only to the amusement of its audience. And moreover it is the causes, not the effects, which are to be exaggerated. That is to say, granted the causes, the effects are to be perfectly natural. It is apparent upon this definition that *The Comedy of Errors* is a perfect Farce. It ravages possibility and outrages our reason. Everybody knows that two persons coming from two different civilizations could not be dressed exactly alike. And when we add that each has a servant, and that the two servants are dressed exactly alike and speak exactly alike, the absurdity goes beyond the balk of unreason itself. But, granted the possibility, everything would then occur as it does in *The Comedy of Errors*.—MORGAN, *The Comedy of Errors* in the *Bankside Shakespeare*.

PLAUSIBILITY OF THE PLOT'S DEVELOPMENT

Only the rough outlines of the play are taken from Plautus; and the motive, the possibility of incessant confusion between two masters and two servants, is manipulated with a skill and certainty which astound us in a beginner, and sometimes with quite irresistible whimsicality. No doubt the merry play is founded upon an extreme improbability. So exact is the mutual resemblance of each pair of twins, no less in clothing than in feature, that not a single person for a moment doubts their identity. Astonishing resemblances between twins do, however, occur in real life; and when once we have accepted the premises, the consequences develop naturally, or at any rate plausibly. We may even say that in the art of intrigue-spinning, which was afterwards somewhat foreign and unattractive to him, the poet here shows himself scarcely inferior to the Spaniards of his own or of a later day, remarkable as was their dexterity.—BRANDES, *William Shakespeare.*

The myriad-minded man, our, and all men's, Shakespeare, has in this piece presented us with a legitimate farce in exactest consonance with the philosophical principles and character of farce, as distinguished from comedy and from entertainments. A proper farce is mainly distinguished from comedy by the license allowed, and even required, in the fable, in order to produce strange and laughable situations. The story need not be probable, it is enough that it is possible. A comedy would scarcely allow even the two Antipholuses; because, although there have been instances of almost indistinguishable likeness in two persons, yet these are mere individual accidents, *casus ludentis naturæ,* and the *verum* will not excuse the *inverisimile.* But farce dares add the two Dromios, and is justified in so doing by the laws of its end and constitution. In a word, farces commence in a postulate, which must be granted.—COLERIDGE, *Lectures on Shakespeare.*

BACKGROUND OF THE PLAY

But whatever skilful management in respect to the plot may be wanting, this scarcely weighs in the balance when

we see how the poet has given the extravagant matter of
these mistakes and intricacies an inner relation to the character of the family in which he has placed them. These
comic parts appear upon a thoroughly tragic background,
which does not interfere at all with the extravagant scenes
in the foreground, and perhaps only makes them the more
conspicuous, but which nevertheless ever appears with sufficient importance to keep under the superficial and weak
impression of a mere farce, the whole substance of which
consisted in the mistakes of those similar twins. The hos-
tilities between Syracuse and Ephesus form the farthest
chiaroscuro background, upon which the whole picture is
drawn, the comic parts of which can scarcely be considered
more fascinating and exciting than the tragic. The fate
of the imprisoned father who is seeking his lost sons, and
who, engaged on a work of love, is condemned to death;
whose mental sufferings at last increase to such a degree,
that he sees himself unknown by his recovered son and believes himself disowned by him; all this raises the piece far
above the character of a mere farce. This tragic part is
united with the comic by the most delicate links—links
which the poet has interwoven into the transmitted story,
according to his subsequent habit, with that totality of his
spiritual nature, that we are absolutely left in doubt as to
whether he acted from blind instinct or with perfect consciousness.—GERVINUS, *Shakespeare's Commentaries.*

THE COMEDY OF ERRORS

DRAMATIS PERSONÆ

Solinus, *duke of Ephesus*
Ægeon, *a merchant of Syracuse*
Antipholus of Ephesus, ⎱ *twin brothers and sons to*
Antipholus of Syracuse, ⎰ *Ægeon and Æmilia*
Dromio of Ephesus, ⎱ *twin brothers, and attendants*
Dromio of Syracuse, ⎰ *on the two Antipholuses*
Balthazar, *a merchant*
Angelo, *a goldsmith*
First Merchant, *friend to Antipholus of Syracuse*
Second Merchant, *to whom Angelo is a debtor*
Pinch, *a schoolmaster*

Æmilia, *wife to Ægeon, an Abbess at Ephesus*
Adriana, *wife to Antipholus of Ephesus*
Luciana, *her sister*
Luce, *servant to Adriana*
A Courtezan

Jailer, Officers, and other Attendants

SYNOPSIS

By J. Ellis Burdick

ACT I

Solinus, Duke of Ephesus, condemns Ægeon, a merchant of Syracuse, to death in accordance with the laws of Ephesus and in default of ransom. Being pressed by the Duke Ægeon tells the story of his life. He was born at Syracuse and brought up as a merchant. Several years before he had been obliged to go to Epidamnum. In that place there was born to him and his wife Æmilia twin sons, "the one so like the other as could not be distinguished." At the same inn and at the same hour a poor woman gave birth to two sons both alike. These boys he had bought to attend his sons. Shortly after, he and his family started for home. They were shipwrecked and the father and mother were separated, each having one son and one slave. Ægeon and the two children with him reached Syracuse, where they lived eighteen years, hearing nothing in that time of the others. Then the son begged permission from his father to take his slave and go in search of his mother and brother. Two years went by and the father heard nothing from this last son; then he, too, started to search for his missing family. Five years had he now "spent in farthest Greece, roaming clean through the bounds of Asia, and coasting homeward, came to Ephesus; hopeless to find, yet loath to leave unsought or that, or any place that harbors men." The Duke, wishing that he might release Ægeon after hearing his sad story, grants him a day's reprieve in order that he might if possible borrow the money for his ransom.

Unknown to Ægeon and unknown to each other, both

the sons and their slaves are in the city of Ephesus
Antipholus of Syracuse has just arrived, and being told b;
a friend that a merchant of Syracuse has been apprehende
and condemned to death, announces that he is from Epi
damnum. The other son has his home in Ephesus and i
in great favor with the Duke, who had married him t
Adriana, a lady of rank. Dromio of Ephesus is sent b;
his mistress to summon his master to dinner and meetin;
Antipholus of Syracuse delivers the message to him. Anti
pholus, thinking it is his own slave joking with him, beat
him.

ACT II

Adriana, after listening to the slave's story of his mas
ter's actions, herself goes to seek him. She meets An
tipholus of Syracuse and makes the same error as to hi
identity, but she succeeds in persuading him to accompan;
her home to dinner. Dromio of Syracuse is set to guar
the gate and to deny entrance to all visitors.

ACT III

Antipholus of Ephesus returns home accompanied b;
Balthazar and is angry to find that he cannot enter hi
own house, but he is persuaded by his friend to go to a
inn for dinner and to return later in the evening. Withi
the house Antipholus of Syracuse protests that some mis
take has been made and addresses pretty speeches to Lu
ciana, sister of Adriana, instead of to Adriana. Dromi
of Syracuse is also claimed as a husband by the kitchen
maid. A tradesman, Angelo by name, confuses the tw
Antipholuses and delivers a gold chain to the Syracusa
which had been ordered by the Ephesian.

ACT IV

Antipholus of Ephesus is arrested for refusing to pa;
for the chain, and meeting Dromio of Syracuse as he i
being led to jail, he sends him to his home for money

Dromio of Syracuse gets the money but in returning with it falls in with his own master and gives it to him. The two Syracusans, believing themselves bewitched, prepare for a hasty departure. Adriana believes her husband and his slave to be mad and has them placed under restraint.

ACT V

Two merchants and Adriana, seeing Antipholus and Dromio of Syracuse on the street, believe them to be the Ephesians, and they are obliged to seek sanctuary in a priory. The abbess protects them. Adriana resolves to complain to the Duke and ask him to force the abbess to yield her husband to her. The Duke is passing just at this time on his way with Ægeon to the place of execution, where the latter is to pay the death penalty. While Adriana is speaking to the Duke, Antipholus and Dromio of Ephesus, having escaped from their captors, rush up and call upon the Duke to do them justice. Ægeon thinks these are the son and slave whom he had brought up and is surprised when he is not recognized. At this moment the abbess and the Syracusans come from the priory and the errors are straightened out. The abbess proves to be Ægeon's long-lost wife, Æmilia. Antipholus of Ephesus is reconciled to his wife, and Antipholus of Syracuse renews his suit with Adriana's sister. The Dromios rejoice over their reunion.

THE COMEDY OF ERRORS

ACT FIRST

Scene I

A hall in the Duke's palace.

Enter Duke, Ægeon, Jailer, Officers, and other Attendants.

Æge. Proceed, Solinus, to procure my fall,
 And by the doom of death end woes and all.
Duke. Merchant of Syracuse, plead no more;
 I am not partial to infringe our laws:
 The enmity and discord which of late
 Sprung from the rancorous outrage of your
 duke
 To merchants, our well-dealing countrymen,
 Who, wanting guilders to redeem their lives,
 Have seal'd his rigorous statutes with their
 bloods,
 Excludes all pity from our threatening looks.
 For, since the mortal and intestine jars   11
 'Twixt thy seditious countrymen and us
 It hath in solemn synods been decreed

---

8. A *guilder* was a coin valued from one shilling and sixpence to
two shillings.—H. N. H.

Both by the Syracusians and ourselves,
To admit no traffic to our adverse towns:
Nay, more,
If any born at Ephesus be seen
At any Syracusian marts and fairs;
Again: if any Syracusian born
Come to the bay of Ephesus, he dies,   20
His goods confiscate to the duke's dispose;
Unless a thousand marks be levied,
To quit the penalty and to ransom him.
Thy substance, valued at the highest rate,
Cannot amount unto a hundred marks;
Therefore by law thou art condemn'd to die.

Æge. Yet this my comfort: when your words are
      done,
My woes end likewise with the evening sun.

Duke. Well, Syracusian, say, in brief, the cause
Why thou departed'st from thy native home, 30
And for what cause thou camest to Ephesus.

Æge. A heavier task could not have been imposed
Than I to speak my griefs unspeakable:
Yet, that the world may witness that my end
Was wrought by nature, not by vile offense,
I'll utter what my sorrow gives me leave.
In Syracusa was I born; and wed
Unto a woman, happy but for me,
And by me, had not our hap been bad.
With her I lived in joy; our wealth increased 40
By prosperous voyages I often made
To Epidamnum; till my factor's death,
And the great care of goods at random left,

42. *"Epidamnum."* The Ff. have *Epidamium*, but this is less

8

Drew me from kind embracements of my
    spouse:
From whom my absence was not six months old,
Before herself, almost at fainting under
The pleasing punishment that women bear,
Had made provision for her following me,
And soon and safe arrived where I was.
There had she not been long but she became 50
A joyful mother of two goodly sons;
And, which was strange, the one so like the
    other
As could not be distinguish'd but by names.
That very hour, and in the self-same inn,
A meaner woman was delivered
Of such a burthen, male twins, both alike:
Those, for their parents were exceeding poor,
I bought, and brought up to attend my sons.
My wife, not meanly proud of two such boys,
Made daily motions for our home return: 60
Unwilling I agreed; alas! too soon
We came aboard.
A league from Epidamnum had we sail'd,
Before the always-wind-obeying deep
Gave any tragic instance of our harm:
But longer did we not retain much hope;
For what obscured light the heavens did grant
Did but convey unto our fearful minds
A doubtful warrant of immediate death;
Which though myself would gladly have em-
    braced,   70

kely to be Shakespeare's form than Epidamnum, which is used in
arner's translation of the *Menœchmi.*—C. H. H.

Yet the incessant weepings of my wife,
Weeping before for what she saw must come,
And piteous plainings of the pretty babes,
That mourn'd for fashion, ignorant what to
    fear,
Forced me to seek delays for them and me.
And this it was, for other means was none:
The sailors sought for safety by our boat,
And left the ship, then sinking-ripe, to us:
My wife, more careful for the latter-born,
Had fasten'd him unto a small spare mast,   80
Such as seafaring men provide for storms;
To him one of the other twins was bound,
Whilst I had been like heedful of the other:
The children thus disposed, my wife and I,
Fixing our eyes on whom our care was fix'd,
Fasten'd ourselves at either end the mast;
And floating straight, obedient to the stream,
Was carried towards Corinth, as we thought.
At length the sun, gazing upon the earth,
Dispersed those vapors that offended us;   90
And, by the benefit of his wished light,
The seas wax'd calm, and we discovered
Two ships from far making amain to us,
Of Corinth that, of Epidaurus this:
But ere they came,—O, let me say no more!
Gather the sequel by that went before.

79. *"The latter-born";* line 125 below seems to imply that th[i]
should be "elder-born," a change adopted by Rowe; but probabl[y]
"the children became exchanged in the confusion during the break[-]
ing-up of the ship."—I. G.

Duke. Nay, forward, old man; do not break off
   so;
   For we may pity, though not pardon thee.
Æge. O, had the gods done so, I had not now
   Worthily term'd them merciless to us!   100
   For, ere the ships could meet by twice five
      leagues,
   We were encounter'd by a mighty rock;
   Which being violently borne upon,
   Our helpful ship was splitted in the midst;
   So that, in this unjust divorce of us,
   Fortune had left to both of us alike
   What to delight in, what to sorrow for.
   Her part, poor soul! seeming as burdened
   With lesser weight, but not with lesser woe,
   Was carried with more speed before the wind;
   And in our sight they three were taken up   111
   By fishermen of Corinth, as we thought.
   At length, another ship had seized on us;
   And, knowing whom it was their hap to save,
   Gave healthful welcome to their shipwreck'd
      guests;
   And would have reft the fishers of their prey,
   Had not their bark been very slow of sail;
   And therefore homeward did they bend their
      course.
   Thus have you heard me sever'd from my bliss;
   That by misfortunes was my life prolong'd, 120
   To tell sad stories of my own mishaps.
Duke. And, for the sake of them thou sorrowest
      for,
   Do me the favor to dilate at full

What hath befall'n of them and thee till now.
Æge. My youngest boy, and yet my eldest care,
    At eighteen years became inquisitive
    After his brother: and importuned me
    That his attendant—so his case was like,
    Reft of his brother, but retain'd his name—
    Might bear him company in the quest of him:
    Whom whilst I labor'd of a love to see,   131
    I hazarded the loss of whom I loved.
    Five summers have I spent in farthest Greece,
    Roaming clean through the bounds of Asia,
    And, coasting homeward, came to Ephesus;
    Hopeless to find, yet loath to leave unsought
    Or that, or any place that harbors men.
    But here must end the story of my life;
    And happy were I in my timely death,
    Could all my travels warrant me they live.   140
Duke. Hapless Ægeon, whom the fates have
        mark'd
    To bear the extremity of dire mishap!
    Now, trust me, were it not against our laws,
    Against my crown, my oath, my dignity,
    Which princes, would they, may not disannul,
    My soul should sue as advocate for thee.
    But, though thou art adjudged to the death,
    And passed sentence may not be recall'd
    But to our honor's great disparagement,
    Yet will I favor thee in what I can.   150
    Therefore, merchant, I'll limit thee this day
    To seek thy help by beneficial help:
    Try all the friends thou hast in Ephesus;
    Beg thou, or borrow, to make up the sum,

And live; if no, then thou art doom'd to die.
Jailer, take him to thy custody.

Jail. I will, my lord.

Æge. Hopeless and helpless doth Ægeon wend,
But to procrastinate his lifeless end. [*Exeunt.*

SCENE II

The Mart.

Enter Antipholus of Syracuse, Dromio of Syracuse, and First Merchant.

First Mer. Therefore give out you are of Epi-
damnum,
Lest that your goods too soon be confiscate.
This very day a Syracusian merchant
Is apprehended for arrival here;
And, not being able to buy out his life,
According to the statute of the town,
Dies ere the weary sun set in the west.
There is your money that I had to keep.

Ant. S. Go bear it to the Centaur, where we host,
And stay there, Dromio, till I come to thee. 10
Within this hour it will be dinner-time:
Till that, I 'll view the manners of the town,
Peruse the traders, gaze upon the buildings,
And then return, and sleep within mine inn;
For with long travel I am stiff and weary.
Get thee away.

Dro. S. Many a man would take you at your word,
And go indeed, having so good a mean. [*Exit.*

13

Ant. S. A trusty villain, sir; that very oft,
    When I am dull with care and melancholy,   2
    Lightens my humor with his merry jests.
    What, will you walk with me about the town,
    And then go to my inn, and dine with me?
First Mer. I am invited, sir, to certain merchants
    Of whom I hope to make much benefit;
    I crave your pardon. Soon at five o'clock,
    Please you, I 'll meet with you upon the mart
    And afterward consort you till bed-time:
    My present business calls me from you now.
Ant. S. Farewell till then: I will go lose myself
    And wander up and down to view the city.   3.
First Mer. Sir, I commend you to your own con
      tent.   [*Exit*
Ant. S. He that commends me to mine own con
      tent
    Commends me to the thing I cannot get.
    I to the world am like a drop of water,
    That in the ocean seeks another drop;
    Who, falling there to find his fellow forth,
    Unseen, inquisitive, confounds himself:
    So I, to find a mother and a brother,
    In quest of them, unhappy, lose myself.   4C

Enter Dromio of Ephesus.

Here comes the almanac of my true date.
What now? how chance thou art return'd so
    soon?

41. *"The almanac of my true date,"* because both were born in
the same hour.--I. G.

Dro. E. Return'd so soon! rather approach'd too
    late:
    The capon burns, the pig falls from the spit;
    The clock hath strucken twelve upon the bell;
    My mistress made it one upon my cheek:
    She is so hot, because the meat is cold;
    The meat is cold, because you come not home;
    You come not home, because you have no
        stomach;
    You have no stomach, having broke your fast;
    But we, that know what 'tis to fast and pray, 51
    Are penitent for your default to-day.
Ant. S. Stop in your wind, sir: tell me this, I pray:
    Where have you left the money that I gave
        you?
Dro. E. O,—sixpence, that I had o' Wednesday
    last
    To pay the saddler for my mistress' crupper?
    The saddler had it, sir; I kept it not.
Ant. S. I am not in a sportive humor now:
    Tell me, and dally not, where is the money?
    We being strangers here, how darest thou trust
    So great a charge from thine own custody? 61
Dro. E. I pray you, jest, sir, as you sit at dinner:
    I from my mistress come to you in post;
    If I return, I shall be post indeed,
    For she will score your fault upon my pate.
    Methinks your maw, like mine, should be your
        clock,

64. *"I shall be post indeed"*; a post stood in the middle of the
shop, on which the scores of the customers were *scored,* or marked
with chalk or notches.—I. G.

66. *"Clock";* Pope's emendation for *"cook,"* the reading of the
Folios.—I. G.

    And strike you home without a messenger.

Ant. S. Come, Dromio, come, these jests are out
        of season;

    Reserve them till a merrier hour than this.

    Where is the gold I gave in charge to thee?   70

Dro. E. To me, sir? why, you gave no gold to me.

Ant. S. Come on, sir knave, have done your fool-
        ishness,

    And tell me how thou hast disposed thy charge.

Dro. E. My charge was but to fetch you from the
        mart

    Home to your house, the Phœnix, sir, to dinner:

    My mistress and her sister stays for you.

Ant. S. Now, as I am a Christian, answer me,

    In what safe place you have bestow'd my
        money;

    Or I shall break that merry sconce of yours,

    That stands on tricks when I am undisposed: 80

    Where is the thousand marks thou had'st of me?

Dro. E. I have some marks of yours upon my pate,

    Some of my mistress' marks upon my shoul-
        ders;

    But not a thousand marks between you both.

    If I should pay your worship those again,

    Perchance you will not bear them patiently.

Ant. S. Thy mistress' marks? what mistress, slave,
        hast thou?

Dro. E. Your worship's wife, my mistress at the
        Phœnix;

    She that doth fast till you come home to dinner,

    And prays that you will hie you home to dinner.

Ant. S. What, wilt thou flout me thus unto my
     face,   91
     Being forbid?   There, take you that, sir knave.
Dro. E. What mean you, sir? for God's sake hold
     your hands!
     Nay, an you will not, sir, I'll take my heels.
                                      [*Exit.*

Ant. S. Upon my life, by some device or other
     The villain is o'er-raught of all my money.
     They say this town is full of cozenage;
     As, nimble jugglers that deceive the eye,
     Dark-working sorcerers that change the mind,
     Soul-killing witches that deform the body, 100
     Disguised cheaters, prating mountebanks,
     And many such-like liberties of sin:
     If it prove so, I will be gone the sooner.
     I'll to the Centaur, to go seek this slave;
     I greatly fear my money is not safe.   [*Exit.*

VI—2

ACT SECOND

Scene I

The house of Antipholus of Ephesus.

Enter Adriana and Luciana.

Adr. Neither my husband nor the slave return'd,
    That in such haste I sent to seek his master!
    Sure, Luciana, it is two o'clock.

Luc. Perhaps some merchant hath invited him,
    And from the mart he's somewhere gone to
      dinner.
    Good sister, let us dine, and never fret:
    A man is master of his liberty:
    Time is their master; and when they see time,
    They'll go or come: if so, be patient, sister.

Adr. Why should their liberty than ours be more?

Luc. Because their business still lies out o' door. 11

Adr. Look, when I serve him so, he takes it ill.

Luc. O, know he is the bridle of your will.

Adr. There's none but asses will be bridled so.

Luc. Why, headstrong liberty is lash'd with woe.
    There's nothing situate under heaven's eye
    But hath his bound, in earth, in sea, in sky:
    The beasts, the fishes, and the winged fowls,
    Are their males' subjects and at their controls:
    Men more divine, the masters of all these,   20

18

Lords of the wide world and wild watery seas,
Indued with intellectual sense and souls,
Of more pre-eminence than fish and fowls,
Are masters to their females, and their lords:
Then let your will attend on their accords.

Adr. This servitude makes you to keep unwed.

Luc. Not this, but troubles of the marriage-bed.

Adr. But, were you wedded, you would bear some
    sway.

Luc. Ere I learn love, I 'll practise to obey.

Adr. How if your husband start some other where?

Luc. Till he come home again, I would forbear. 31

Adr. Patience unmoved! no marvel though she
    pause;
They can be meek that have no other cause.
A wretched soul, bruised with adversity,
We bid be quiet when we hear it cry;
But were we burden'd with like weight of pain,
As much, or more, we should ourselves com-
    plain:
So thou, that hast no unkind mate to grieve
    thee,
With urging helpless patience wouldst relieve
    me;
But, if thou live to see like right bereft,   40
This fool-begg'd patience in thee will be left.

41. Probably meaning a patience so foolish as to cause one to be
begged for a fool; referring to the old custom of soliciting the
guardianship of fools and idiotic persons with a view to come at
their revenues. The king, being the legal guardian of such persons,
might make over the trust to whom he pleased; and relatives or
other interested parties would beg the office, and, no doubt, often
made or imagined the folly they wanted to have the care of. See
Love's Labour's Lost, Act v. sc. 2, note 31.—H. N. H.

Luc. Well, I will marry one day, but to try.
   Here comes your man; now is your husband
     nigh.

Enter Dromio of Ephesus.

Adr. Say, is your tardy master now at hand?

Dro. E. Nay, he's at two hands with me, and
   that my two ears can witness.

Adr. Say, didst thou speak with him? know'st thou
   his mind?

Dro. E. Aye, aye, he told his mind upon mine ear:
   Beshrew his hand, I scarce could understand it.

Luc. Spake he so doubtfully, thou couldst not 50
   feel his meaning?

Dro. E. Nay, he struck so plainly, I could too
   well feel his blows; and withal so doubtfully,
   that I could scarce understand them.

Adr. But say, I prithee, is he coming home?
   It seems he hath great care to please his wife.

Dro. E. Why, mistress, sure my master is horn-
    mad.

Adr. Horn-mad, thou villain!

Dro. E.   I mean not cuckold-mad;
   But, sure, he is stark mad.
   When I desired him to come home to dinner, 60
   He ask'd me for a thousand marks in gold:
   ''Tis dinner-time,' quoth I; 'My gold!' quoth
    he:
   'Your meat doth burn,' quoth I; 'My gold!'
    quoth he:
   'Will you come home?' quoth I; 'My gold?'
    quoth he,

'Where is the thousand marks I gave thee, vil-
    lain?'

'The pig,' quoth I, 'is burn'd;' 'My gold!' quoth
    he:

'My mistress, sir,' quoth I; 'Hang up thy mis-
    tress!

I know not thy mistress; out on thy mistress!'

Luc. Quoth who?

Dro. E. Quoth my master: 70

'I know,' quoth he, 'no house, no wife, no mis-
    tress.'

So that my errand, due unto my tongue,

I thank him, I bare home upon my shoulders;

For, in conclusion, he did beat me there.

Adr. Go back again, thou slave, and fetch him
    home.

Dro. E. Go back again, and be new beaten home?

For God's sake, send some other messenger.

Adr. Back, slave, or I will break thy pate across.

Dro. E. And he will bless that cross with other
    beating:

Between you I shall have a holy head.   80

Adr. Hence, prating peasant! fetch thy master
    home.

Dro. E. Am I so round with you as you with me,

That like a football you do spurn me thus?

You spurn me hence, and he will spurn me
    hither:

82. He plays upon the word *round,* which signifies spherical, as
applied to himself; and *free in speech,* as regards his mistress. To
be round with anyone is to be plain spoken.—H. N. H.

  If I last in this service, you must case me in
     leather.   [*Exit.*

Luc. Fie, how impatience loureth in your face!

Adr. His company must do his minions grace,
    Whilst I at home starve for a merry look.
    Hath homely age the alluring beauty took
    From my poor cheek? then he hath wasted it: 90
    Are my discourses dull? barren my wit?
    If voluble and sharp discourse be marr'd,
    Unkindness blunts it more than marble hard:
    Do their gay vestments his affections bait?
    That's not my fault; he's master of my state:
    What ruins are in me that can be found,
    By him not ruin'd? then is he the ground
    Of my defeatures.   My decayed fair
    A sunny look of his would soon repair:
    But, too unruly deer, he breaks the pale,   100
    And feeds from home; poor I am but his stale.

Luc. Self-harming jealousy! fie, beat it hence!

Adr. Unfeeling fools can with such wrongs dis-
     pense.
    I know his eye doth homage otherwhere;
    Or else what lets it but he would be here?
    Sister, you know he promised me a chain;
    Would that alone, alone he would detain,
    So he would keep fair quarter with his bed!
    I see the jewel best enameled
    Will lose his beauty; yet the gold bides still, 110
    That others touch, and often touching will

109–113. These lines read as follows in the Folio:—

    "I see the Iewell best enameled
     Will loose his luster; yet the gold bides still

Wear gold: and no man that hath a name,
By falsehood and corruption doth it shame.
Since that my beauty cannot please his eye,
I'll weep what's left away, and weeping die.
Luc. How many fond fools serve mad jealousy!
                                        [*Exeunt.*

SCENE II

A public place

Enter Antipholus of Syracuse.

Ant. S. The gold I gave to Dromio is laid up
Safe at the Centaur; and the heedful slave
Is wander'd forth, in care to seek me out
By computation and mine host's report.
I could not speak with Dromio since at first
I sent him from the mart.   See, here he comes.

> That others touch, and often touching will,
> Where gold and no man that hath a name," &c

The change of *where* to *wear* in the last line has been generally accepted, as also *and though* for *yet* in the second line; *yet* for *and* in the third; *and so a man* for *and no man* in the fourth; Warburton paraphrases this passage thus emended:—"Gold, indeed, will long bear the handling; however, often *touching* (*i. e.* assaying) will wear even gold; just so the greatest character, though as pure as gold itself, may in time be injured by the repeated attacks of falsehood and corruption." The Cambridge editors wisely abstain from these wholesale emendations, though so far no satisfactory explanation has been given of the lines. May not the meaning of the passage depend on some such interpretation as this:—The wife (the jewel) soon loses her beauty and ceases to attract, but man (the gold) still stands the test, assayed by other women, and although gold wears out if assayed too often, yet a man of good reputation is not shamed by his falsehood and corruption. "Wherefore," says Adriana, "since I (the jewel) cannot please his eye, I'll weep what's left away," &c.—I. G.

Enter Dromio of Syracuse.

How now, sir! is your merry humor alter'd?
As you love strokes, so jest with me again.
You know no Centaur? you received no gold?
Your mistress sent to have me home to din-
ner?   10
My house was at the Phœnix? Wast thou
mad,
That thus so madly thou didst answer me?
Dro. S. What answer, sir? when spake I such a
word?
Ant. S. Even now, even here, not half an hour
since.
Dro. S. I did not see you since you sent me hence,
Home to the Centaur, with the gold you gave
me.
Ant. S. Villain, thou didst deny the gold's receipt,
And told'st me of a mistress and a dinner;
For which, I hope, thou felt'st I was displeased.
Dro. S. I am glad to see you in this merry vein: 20
What means this jest? I pray you, master, tell
me.
Ant. S. Yea, dost thou jeer and flout me in the
teeth?
Think'st thou I jest? Hold, take thou that,
and that. [*Beating him.*
Dro. S. Hold, sir, for God's sake! now your jest is
earnest:
Upon what bargain do you give it me?
Ant. S. Because that I familiarly sometimes
Do use you for my fool, and chat with you,

Your sauciness will jest upon my love,
And make a common of my serious hours.
When the sun shines let foolish gnats make
    sport,   30
But creep in crannies when he hides his beams.
If you will jest with me, know my aspect,
And fashion your demeanor to my looks,
Or I will beat this method in your sconce.

Dro. S. Sconce call you it? so you would leave
battering, I had rather have it a head: an
you use these blows long, I must get a
sconce for my head, and insconce it too; or
else I shall seek my wit in my shoulders.
But, I pray, sir, why am I beaten?   40

Ant. S. Dost thou not know?

Dro. S. Nothing, sir, but that I am beaten.

Ant. S. Shall I tell you why?

Dro. S. Aye, sir, and wherefore; for they say
every why hath a wherefore.

Ant. S. Why, first,—for flouting me; and then,
    wherefore,—
For urging it the second time on me.

Dro. S. Was there ever any man thus beaten out
    of season,
When in the why and the wherefore is neither
    rhyme nor reason?
Well, sir, I thank you.   50

Ant. S. Thank me, sir! for what?

Dro. S. Marry sir, for this something that you
gave me for nothing.

Ant. S. I 'll make you amends next, to give you

nothing for something. But say, sir, is it
dinner-time?

Dro. S. No, sir: I think the meat wants that I
have.

Ant. S. In good time, sir; what's that?

Dro. S. Basting.

Ant. S. Well, sir, then 'twill be dry.   60

Dro. S. If it be, sir, I pray you, eat none of it.

Ant. S. Your reason?

Dro. S. Lest it make you choleric, and purchase
me another dry basting.

Ant. S. Well, sir, learn to jest in good time:
there's a time for all things.

Dro. S. I durst have denied that, before you
were so choleric.

Ant. S. By what rule, sir?

Dro. S. Marry, sir, by a rule as plain as the   70
plain bald pate of father Time himself.

Ant. S. Let's hear it.

Dro. S. There's no time for a man to recover
his hair that grows bald by nature.

Ant. S. May he not do it by fine and recovery?

Dro. S. Yes, to pay a fine for a periwig, and recover the lost hair of another man.

Ant. S. Why is Time such a niggard of hair,
being, as it is, so plentiful an excrement?

Dro. S. Because it is a blessing that he bestows 80
on beasts: and what he hath scanted men in
hair, he hath given them in wit.

Ant. S. Why, but there's many a man hath
more hair than wit.

Dro. S. Not a man of those but he hath the wit
to lose his hair.

Ant. S. Why, thou didst conclude hairy men
plain dealers without wit.

Dro. S. The plainer dealer, the sooner lost: yet
he loseth it in a kind of jollity.   90

Ant. S. For what reason?

Dro. S. For two; and sound ones too.

Ant. S. Nay, not sound, I pray you.

Dro. S. Sure ones, then.

Ant. S. Nay, not sure, in a thing falsing.

Dro. S. Certain ones, then.

Ant. S. Name them.

Dro. S. The one, to save the money that he
spends in tiring; the other, that at dinner
they should not drop in his porridge.   100

Ant. S. You would all this time have proved
there is no time for all things.

Dro. S. Marry, and did, sir; namely, no time
to recover hair lost by nature.

Ant. S. But your reason was not substantial,
why there is no time to recover.

Dro. S. Thus I mend it: Time himself is bald,
and therefore to the world's end will have
bald followers.

Ant. S. I knew 'twould be a bald conclusion: 110
But, soft! who wafts us yonder?

Enter Adriana and Luciana.

90. *"Jollity";* Staunton suggested that the reading is an error for
"policy," and the reading has been adopted by some modern editors.
-I. G.

27

Adr. Aye, aye, Antipholus, look strange and
    frown:
    Some other mistress hath thy sweet aspects;
    I am not Adriana nor thy wife.
    The time was once when thou unurged wouldst
        vow
    That never words were music to thine ear,
    That never object pleasing in thine eye,
    That never touch well welcome to thy hand,
    That never meat sweet-savor'd in thy taste,
    Unless I spake, or look'd, or touch'd, or carved
        to thee.   120
    How comes it now, my husband, O, how comes
        it,
    That thou art then estranged from thyself?
    Thyself I call it, being strange to me,
    That, undividable, incorporate,
    Am better than thy dear selfs better part.
    Ah, do not tear away thyself from me!
    For know, my love, as easy mayst thou fall
    A drop of water in the breaking gulf,
    And take unmingled thence that drop again,
    Without addition or diminishing,   130
    As take from me thyself, and not me too.
    How dearly would it touch thee to the quick,
    Shouldst thou but hear I were licentious,
    And that this body, consecrate to thee,
    By ruffian lust should be contaminate!
    Wouldst thou not spit at me and spurn at me,

---

120. As the line stands, it reads as an Alexandrine. Walker suggested *carv'd thee* for *carved to thee;* others propose the omission of
to thee; neither change seems desirable.—I. G.

And hurl the name of husband in my face,
And tear the stain'd skin off my harlot-brow,
And from my false hand cut the wedding-ring,
And break it with a deep-divorcing vow?   140
I know thou canst; and therefore see thou do it.
I am possess'd with an adulterate blot;
My blood is mingled with the crime of lust:
For if we two be one, and thou play false,
I do digest the poison of thy flesh,
Being strumpeted by thy contagion.
Keep, then, fair league and truce with thy true
    bed;
I live distain'd, thou undishonored.

Ant. S. Plead you to me, fair dame? I know you
    not:
In Ephesus I am but two hours old,   150
As strange unto your town as to your talk;
Who, every word by all my wit being scann'd,
Wants wit in all one word to understand.

Luc. Fie, brother! how the world is changed with
    you!
When were you wont to use my sister thus?
She sent for you by Dromio home to dinner.

Ant. S. By Dromio?

Dro. S. By me?

Adr. By thee; and this thou didst return from him,
That he did buffet thee, and, in his blows,   160

---

148. *"I live distain'd, thou undishonored"*; so read the Folios;
distain'd has been changed to *unstain'd* in most modern editions;
Heath proposed *"I live distained, thou dishonored."* The line as
it stands in the text seems to mean, "I live distained (*i. e.* stained),
if untrue to my marriage vows; you, however, live undishonored,
however false you may be."—I. G.

Denied my house for his, me for his wife.

Ant. S. Did you converse, sir, with this gentle-
      woman?

What is the course and drift of your compact?

Dro. S. I, sir? I never saw her till this time.

Ant. S. Villain, thou liest; for even her very words
Didst thou deliver to me on the mart.

Dro. S. I never spake with her in all my life.

Ant. S. How can she thus then call us by our
      names?

Unless it be by inspiration.

Adr. How ill agrees it with your gravity   170
To counterfeit thus grossly with your slave,
Abetting him to thwart me in my mood!
Be it my wrong you are from me exempt,
But wrong not that wrong with a more con-
      tempt.
Come, I will fasten on this sleeve of thine:
Thou art an elm, my husband, I a vine,
Whose weakness, married to thy stronger state,
Makes me with thy strength to communicate:
If aught possess thee from me, it is dross,
Usurping ivy, brier, or idle moss;   180
Who, all for want of pruning, with intrusion
Infect thy sap, and live on thy confusion.

176. So Milton's Paradise Lost, b. v.: "They led the *vine* to wed
her *elm:* She, spous'd, about him twines her marriageable arms."
Thus also in *A Midsummer-Night's Dream:* "The female ivy so en-
rings the barky fingers of the elm." Mr. Douce observes that there
is something extremely beautiful in making the vine the lawful
spouse of the elm, and the *parasite* plants here named its *concubines.*
See also Ovid's tale of Vertumnus and Pomona.—H. N. H.

Ant. S. To me she speaks; she moves me foɪ her
    theme:
    What, was I married to her in my dream?
    Or sleep I now, and think I hear all this?
    What error drives our eyes and ears amiss?
    Until I know this sure uncertainty,
    I 'll entertain the offer'd fallacy.

Luc. Dromio, go bid the servants spread for din-
    ner.

Dro. S. O, for my beads! I cross me for a sin-
    ner.   190
    This is the fairy land: O spite of spites!
    We talk with goblins, owls, and sprites:
    If we obey them not, this will ensue,
    They 'll suck our breath, or pinch us black and
    blue.

Luc. Why pratest thou to thyself, and answer'st
    not?
    Dromio, thou drone, thou snail, thou slug, thou
    sot!

187. *"this sure uncertainty,"* *i. e.* "This to her surely a thing un-
certain."—I. G.

192. The second Folio reads *"and Elves Sprites,"* which Rowe
altered to *"Elvish sprites,"* a reading adopted by most editors.—I. G.

Theobald changed *owls* to *ouphes* in this passage most unwarrant-
ably. It is those *unlucky birds,* the striges or *screech-owls,* which
are meant. It has been asked, How should Shakespeare know that
screech-owls were considered by the Romans as witches? Do these
cavilers think that Shakespeare never looked into a book? Take an
extract from the *Cambridge Latin Dictionary,* 1594, 8vo., probably
the very book he used: "Strix, a *scritche owle;* an unluckie kind of
bird (as they of old time said) *which sucked out the blood of in-
fants lying in their cradles;* a witch, that changeth the favor of
children; *an hagge or fairie."* So in *The London Prodigal,* a comedy, 1605: "Soul, I think I am sure crossed or *witch'd with an owl."*
—H. N. H.

Dro. S. I am transformed, master, am not I?

Ant. S. I think thou art in mind, and so am I.

Dro. S. Nay, master, both in mind and in my shape.

Ant. S. Thou hast thine own form.

Dro. S.   No, I am an ape.   200

Luc. If thou art changed to aught, 'tis to an ass.

Dro. S. 'Tis true; she rides me, and I long for
    grass.
    'Tis so, I am an ass; else it could never be
    But I should know her as well as she knows me.

Adr. Come, come, no longer will I be a fool,
    To put the finger in the eye and weep,
    Whilst man and master laughs my woes to
      scorn.
    Come, sir, to dinner. Dromio, keep the gate.
    Husband, I'll dine above with you to-day,
    And shrive you of a thousand idle pranks.   210
    Sirrah, if any ask you for your master,
    Say he dines forth, and let no creature enter.
    Come, sister. Dromio, play the porter well.

Ant. S. Am I in earth, in heaven, or in hell?
    Sleeping or waking? mad or well-advised?
    Known unto these, and to myself disguised!
    I'll say as they say, and persever so,
    And in this mist at all adventures go.

Dro. S. Master, shall I be porter at the gate?

Adr. Aye; and let none enter, lest I break your
    pate.   220

Luc. Come, come, Antipholus, we dine too late.

                           [*Exeunt.*

---

201. "'tis to an ass"; the words remind one of Bottom's trans-formation in the *Midsummer Night's Dream.*—I. G.

ACT THIRD

Scene I

Before the house of Antipholus of Ephesus.

Enter Antipholus of Ephesus, Dromio of Ephesus, Angelo, and Balthazar.

Ant. E. Good Signior Angelo, you must excuse
    us all;
  My wife is shrewish when I keep not hours:
  Say that I linger'd with you at your shop
  To see the making of her carcanet,
  And that to-morrow you will bring it home.
  But here 's a villain that would face me down
  He met me on the mart, and that I beat him,
  And charged him with a thousand marks in
    gold,
  And that I did deny my wife and house.
  Thou drunkard, thou, what didst thou mean by
    this?   10

Dro. E. Say what you will, sir, but I know what I
    know;
  That thou beat me at the mart, I have your
    hand to show:
  If the skin were parchment, and the blows you
    gave were ink,
  Your own handwriting would tell you what I
    think.

Ant. E. I think thou art an ass.

Dro. E.   Marry, so it doth appear

By the wrongs I suffer, and the blows I bear.

I should kick, being kick'd; and, being at that
pass,

You would keep from my heels, and beware of
an ass.

Ant. E. You 're sad, Signior Balthazar; pray God
our cheer

May answer my good will and your good welcome here.   20

Bal. I hold your dainties cheap, sir, and your welcome dear.

Ant. E. O, Signior Balthazar, either at flesh or
fish,

A table full of welcome makes scarce one dainty
dish.

Bal. Good meat, sir, is common: that every churl
affords.

Ant. E. And welcome more common; for that 's
nothing but words.

Bal. Small cheer and great welcome makes a merry
feast.

Ant. E. Aye, to a niggardly host and more sparing
guest:

But though my cates be mean, take them in
good part;

Better cheer may you have, but not with better
heart.

But, soft! my door is lock'd.—Go bid them let
us in.   30

Dro. E. Maud, Bridget, Marian, Cicely, Gillian,
    Ginn!

Dro. S. [*Within*] Mome, malt-horse, capon, cox-
    comb, idiot, patch!

    Either get thee from the door, or sit down at
      the hatch.

    Dost thou conjure for wenches, that thou call'st
      for such store,

    When one is one too many?   Go get thee from
      the door.

Dro. E. What patch is made our porter?   My
    master stays in the street.

Dro. S. [*Within*] Let him walk from whence he
    came, lest he catch cold on 's feet.

Ant. E. Who talks within there? ho, open the
    door!

Dro. S. [*Within*] Right, sir; I 'll tell you when,
    an you 'll tell me wherefore.

Ant. E. Wherefore? for my dinner: I have not
    dined to-day.   40

Dro. S. [*Within*] Nor to-day here you must not;
    come again when you may.

Ant. E. What art thou that keepest me out from
    the house I owe?

Dro. S. [*Within*] The porter for this time, sir,
    and my name is Dromio.

Dro. E. O villain, thou hast stolen both mine office
    and my name!

    The one ne'er got me credit, the other mickle
      blame.

---

32. "*patch*," fool. The word was used both with reference to the
motley of a fool or jester, and to patched clothes.—C. H. H.

If thou hadst been Dromio to-day in my place
Thou wouldst have changed thy face for
    name, or thy name for an ass.
Luce. [*Within*] What a coil is there, Dromio
    who are those at the gate!
Dro. E. Let my master in, Luce.
Luce.   [*Within*] 'Faith, no; he comes too late
And so tell your master.
Dro. E.   O Lord, I must laugh!   5
    Have at you with a proverb;—Shall I set in m
        staff?
Luce. [*Within*] Have at you with another
    that 's,—When? can you tell?
Dro. S. [*Within*] If thy name be call'd Luce,—
    Luce, thou hast answer'd him well.
Ant. E. Do you hear, you minion? you 'll let us in
    I hope?
Luce. [*Within*] I thought to have ask'd you.
Dro. S.   [*Within*] And you said no
Dro. E. So, come, help: well struck! there wa
    blow for blow.
Ant. E. Thou baggage, let me in.
Luce. [*Within*] Can you tell for whose sake?

47. *"for an ass."* Collier needlessly altered to *for a face,* partl
on the ground of rhyme. But *ass* in Eliz. Eng. was a passabl
rhyme to *face* (as to *ace* which often contains a pun on *ass*)
Dromio means that if Dromio S. had been in his place when h
was flogged, instead of stealing the name Dromio he would hav
been glad to get rid of it, or else have proved himself an ass.—C. F
H.

53. *"If thy name be called Luce": "Luce"="pike";* there is per
haps a play upon "pike" in the sense of "spear," *cp. "Shall I set i
my staff?"* line 51.—I. G.

54. Probably a line has been lost rhyming with this; the rhymin
word was perhaps *rope.*—I. G.

Dro. E. Master, knock the door hard.

Luce.   [*Within*] Let him knock till it ache.

Ant. E. You 'll cry for this, minion, if I beat the
   door down.

Luce. [*Within*] What needs all that, and a pair
   of stocks in the town?   60

Adr. [*Within*] Who is that at the door that keeps
   all this noise?

Dro. S. [*Within*] By my troth, your town is
   troubled with unruly boys.

Ant. E. Are you there, wife? you might have come
   before.

Adr. [*Within*] Your wive, sir knave! go get you
   from the door.

Dro. E. If you went in pain, master, this 'knave'
   would go sore.

Ang. Here is neither cheer, sir, nor welcome: we
   would fain have either.

Bal. In debating which was best, we shall part with
   neither.

Dro. E. They stand at the door, master; bid them
   welcome hither.

Ant. E. There is something in the wind, that we
   cannot get in.

Dro. E. You would say so, master, if your gar-
   ments were thin.   70
   Your cake here is warm within; you stand here
      in the cold:
   It would make a man mad as a buck, to be so
      bought and sold.

Ant. E. Go fetch me something: I 'll break ope
   the gate.

Dro. S. [*Within*] Break any breaking here, and
 I 'll break your knave's pate.

Dro. E. A man may break a word with you, sir
 and words are but wind;

Aye, and break it in your face, so he break i
 not behind.

Dro. S. [*Within*] It seems thou want'st breaking
 out upon thee, hind!

Dro. E. Here 's too much 'out upon thee!' I pray
 thee, let me in.

Dro. S. [*Within*] Aye, when fowls have no feath
 ers, and fish have no fin.

Ant. E. Well, I 'll break in: go borrow me a crow

Dro. E. A crow without feather? Master, mean
 you so?   81

For a fish without a fin, there 's a fowl withou
 a feather:

If a crow help us in, sirrah, we 'll pluck a crow
 together.

Ant. E. Go get thee gone; fetch me an iron crow

Bal. Have patience, sir: O, let it not be so!

Herein you war against your reputation,

And draw within the compass of suspect

The unviolated honor of your wife.

Once this,—your long experience of her wis
 dom,

Her sober virtue, years, and modesty, 90

Plead on her part some cause to you unknown

And doubt not, sir, but she will well excuse

Why at this time the doors are made against
 you.

Be ruled by me: depart in patience,

And let us to the Tiger all to dinner;
And about evening come yourself alone
To know the reason of this strange restraint.
If by strong hand you offer to break in
Now in the stirring passage of the day,
A vulgar comment will be made of it,   100
And that supposed by the common rout
Against your yet ungalled estimation,
That may with foul intrusion enter in,
And dwell upon your grave when you are dead;
For slander lives upon succession,
For ever housed where it gets possession.

Ant. E. You have prevail'd: I will depart in quiet,
And, in despite of mirth, mean to be merry.
I know a wench of excellent discourse,
Pretty and witty; wild, and yet, too, gentle: 110
There will we dine. This woman that I mean,
My wife—but, I protest, without desert—
Hath oftentimes upbraided me withal:
To her will we to dinner. [*To Ang.*] Get you
    home,
And fetch the chain; by this I know 'tis made:
Bring it, I pray you, to the Porpentine;
For there 's the house: that chain I will be-
    stow—
Be it for nothing but to spite my wife—
Upon mine hostess there: good sir, make haste.
Since mine own doors refuse to entertain me, 120
I 'll knock elsewhere, to see if they 'll disdain
    me.

108. One would suppose it should be in despite of *grief:* but the
man is in a state of mind, that *mirth* is *grievous* to him.—H. N. H.

39

Ang. I 'll meet you at that place some hour hence
Ant. E. Do so. [This jest shall cost me some ex
    pense.   [*Exeunt*

Scene II

The same.

Enter Luciana, with Antipholus of Syracuse.

Luc. And may it be that you have quite forgot
    A husband's office? shall, Antipholus,
Even in the spring of love, thy love-spring
    rot?
    Shall love, in building, grow so ruinous?
If you did wed my sister for her wealth,
    Then for her wealth's sake use her with mor
        kindness:
Or if you like elsewhere, do it by stealth;
    Muffle your false love with some show o
        blindness:
Let not my sister read it in your eye;
    Be not thy tongue thy own shame's orator; 1
Look sweet, speak fair, become disloyalty;
    Apparel vice like virtue's harbinger;
Bear a fair presence, though your heart b
    tainted;
    Teach sin the carriage of a holy saint;
Be secret-false: what need she be acquainted?
    What simple thief brags of his own attaint?
'Tis double wrong, to truant with your bed,
    And let her read it in thy looks at board:

Shame hath a bastard fame, well managed;
  Ill deeds are doubled with an evil word.   20
Alas, poor women! make us but believe,
  Being compact of credit, that you love us;
Though others have the arm, show us the sleeve;
  We in your motion turn, and you may move
    us.
Then, gentle brother, get you in again;
  Comfort my sister, cheer her, call her wife;
'Tis holy sport, to be a little vain,
  When the sweet breath of flattery conquers
    strife.
Ant. S. Sweet mistress,—what your name is else,
    I know not,
  Nor by what wonder you do hit of mine,— 30
Less in your knowledge and your grace you
    show not
  Than our earth's wonder; more than earth
    divine.
Teach me, dear creature, how to think and
    speak;
  Lay open to my earthy-gross conceit,
Smother'd in errors, feeble, shallow, weak,
  The folded meaning of your words' deceit.
Against my soul's pure truth why labor you
  To make it wander in an unknown field?
Are you a god? would you create me new?
  Transform me, then, and to your power I 'll
    yield.   40
But if that I am I, then well I know
  Your weeping sister is no wife of mine,

Nor to her bed no homage do I owe:
  Far more, far more to you do I decline.
O, train me not, sweet mermaid, with thy note,
  To drown me in thy sister's flood of tears:
Sing, siren, for thyself, and I will dote:
  Spread o'er the silver waves thy golden hairs,
And as a bed I 'll take them, and there lie;
  And, in that glorious supposition, think   50
He gains by death that hath such means to die:
  Let Love, being light, be drowned if she
    sink!

Luc. What, are you mad, that you do reason so?

Ant. S. Not mad, but mated; how, I do not know.

Luc. It is a fault that springeth from your eye.

Ant. S. For gazing on your beams, fair sun, being
  by.

Luc. Gaze where you should, and that will clear
  your sight.

Ant. S. As good to wink, sweet love, as look on
  night.

Luc. Why call you me love? call my sister so.

Ant. S. Thy sister's sister.

Luc.   That's my sister.

Ant. S.   No;   60
It is thyself, mine own self's better part,
  Mine eye's clear eye, my dear heart's dearer
    heart,
My food, my fortune, and my sweet hope's aim,
  My sole earth's heaven, and my heaven's claim.

---

54. *"Mated"* means *matched with a wife,* and *confounded.* A quibble is intended.—H. N. H.

Luc. All this my sister is, or else should be.

Ant. S. Call thyself sister, sweet, for I am thee.
     Thee will I love, and with thee lead my life:
     Thou hast no husband yet, nor I no wife.
     Give me thy hand.

Luc.   O, soft, sir! hold you still:
     I'll fetch my sister, to get her good will.   70

                           [*Exit.*

Enter Dromio of Syracuse.

Ant. S. Why, how now, Dromio! where runn'st
     thou so fast?

Dro. S. Do you know me, sir? am I Dromio?
     am I your man? am I myself?

Ant. S. Thou art Dromio, thou art my man,
     thou art thyself.

Dro. S. I am an ass, I am a woman's man, and
     besides myself.

Ant. S. What woman's man? and how besides
     thyself?   80

Dro. S. Marry, sir, besides myself, I am due to
     a woman; one that claims me, one that
     haunts me, one that will have me.

Ant. S. What claim lays she to thee?

Dro. S. Marry, sir, such claim as you would lay
     to your horse; and she would have me as a
     beast: not that, I being a beast, she would
     have me; but that she, being a very beastly
     creature, lays claim to me.

66. *"I am thee";* this reading of the Folio may surely, without
risk, be emended:—*"I aim thee,"* i. e. *"I aim at thee";* the transitive
use of *aim* is found in Elizabethan writers.—I. G.

Ant. S. What is she?

Dro. S. A very reverent body; aye, such a one
as a man may not speak of, without he say
Sir-reverence. I have but lean luck in the
match, and yet is she a wondrous fat marriage.

Ant. S. How dost thou mean a fat marriage?

Dro. S. Marry, sir, she 's the kitchen-wench,
and all grease; and I know not what use to
put her to, but to make a lamp of her, and
run from her by her own light. I warrant, 10(
her rags, and the tallow in them, will burn a
Poland winter; if she lives till doomsday,
she 'll burn a week longer than the whole
world.

Ant. S. What complexion is she of?

Dro. S. Swart, like my shoe, but her face nothing like so clean kept: for why she sweats;
a man may go over shoes in the grime of it.

Ant. S. That 's a fault that water will mend.

Dro. S. No, sir, 'tis in grain; Noah's flood could 11(
not do it.

Ant. S. What 's her name?

Dro. S. Nell, sir; but her name and three quarters, that 's an ell and three quarters, will not
measure her from hip to hip.

Ant. S. Then she bears some breadth?

Dro. S. No longer from head to foot than from

114. Of course there is a quibble between *a Nell* and *an ell;* re
ferring to an ell Flemish, which is three quarters of a yard.—
H. N. H.

hip to hip: she is spherical, like a globe; I
could find out countries in her.

Ant. S. In what part of the body stands Ire- 120
land?

Dro. S. Marry, sir, in her buttocks: I found it
out by the bogs.

Ant. S. Where Scotland?

Dro. S. I found it by the barrenness; hard in
the palm of the hand.

Ant. S. Where France?

Dro. S. In her forehead; armed and reverted,
making war against her heir.

Ant. S. Where England? 130

Dro. S. I looked for the chalky cliffs, but I
could find no whiteness in them; but I guess
it stood in her chin, by the salt rheum that
ran between France and it.

Ant. S. Where Spain?

Dro. S. 'Faith, I saw it not; but I felt it hot in
her breath.

Ant. S. Where America, the Indies?

129. *"armed and reverted, making war against her heir";* Folio 2
substituted *hair* for *heir,* but the play upon words is the whole point
of the passage, an allusion being intended to the War of the League
against Henry of Navarre, the heir of Henry III of France, whose
cause was supported by Elizabeth; in 1591 she sent a body of 4,000
men under Essex to help him. "Mistress Nell's brazen forehead
seemed to push back her rough and rebellious hair, as France resisted the claim of the Protestant heir to the throne."—Clarke.

English enthusiasm for Henry of Navarre found expression, too,
in Shakespeare's *Love's Labor's Lost.*

As regards the peculiar use of *reverted, i. e.* "turned back,"
Schmidt suggests that there may be a play upon the sense of
"fallen to another proprietor."—I. G.

Dro. S. Oh, sir, upon her nose, all o'er embel-
    lished with rubies, carbuncles, sapphires, de- 140
    clining their rich aspect to the hot breath of
    Spain; who sent whole armadoes of caracks
    to be ballast at her nose.

Ant. S. Where stood Belgia, the Netherlands?

Dro. S. Oh, sir, I did not look so low.   To con-
    clude, this drudge, or diviner, laid claim to
    me; called me Dromio; swore I was assured
    to her; told me what privy marks I had
    about me, as, the mark of my shoulder, the
    mole in my neck, the great wart on my left 150
    arm, that I, amazed, ran from her as a witch:
    And, I think, if my breast had not been made
        of faith, and my heart of steel,
    She had transform'd me to a curtal dog,
        and made me turn i' the wheel.

Ant. S. Go hie thee presently, post to the road:
    An if the wind blow any way from shore,
    I will not harbor in this town to-night:
    If any bark put forth, come to the mart,
    Where I will walk till thou return to me.
    If every one knows us, and we know none,   159
    'Tis time, I think, to trudge, pack, and be gone.

Dro. S. As from a bear a man would run for life,
    So fly I from her that would be my wife.
                           [*Exit.*

Ant. S. There's none but witches do inhabit here;
    And therefore 'tis high time that I were hence.
    She that doth call me husband, even my soul

152. Alluding to the popular belief that a great share of *faith* was
a protection from witchcraft.—H. N. H.

Doth for a wife abhor.   But her fair sister,
Possess'd with such a gentle sovereign grace,
Of such enchanting presence and discourse,
Hath almost made me traitor to myself:
But, lest myself be guilty to self-wrong,   170
I 'll stop mine ears against the mermaid's song.

Enter Angelo with the chain.

Ang. Master Antipholus,—

Ant. S.   Aye, that 's my name.

Ang. I know it well, sir: lo, here is the chain.
I thought to have ta'en you at the Porpentine:
The chain unfinish'd made me stay thus long.

Ant. S. What is your will that I shall do with this?

Ang. What please yourself, sir: I have made it for
    you.

Ant. S. Made it for me, sir! I bespoke it not.

Ang. Not once, nor twice, but twenty times you
    have.   179
Go home with it, and please your wife withal;
And soon at supper-time I 'll visit you,
And then receive my money for the chain.

Ant. S. I pray you, sir, receive the money now,
For fear you ne'er see chain nor money more.

Ang. You are a merry man, sir: fare you well.

                                        [*Exit.*

Ant. S. What I should think of this, I cannot tell:
But this I think, there 's no man is so vain
That would refuse so fair an offer'd chain.
I see a man here needs not live by shifts,   189
When in the streets he meets such golden gifts.
I 'll to the mart, and there for Dromio stay:
If any ship put out, then straight away. [*Exit.*

ACT FOURTH

SCENE I

A public place.

Enter Second Merchant, Angelo, and an Officer.

Sec. Mer. You know since Pentecost the sum is
    due,
    And since I have not much importuned you;
    Nor now I had not, but that I am bound
    To Persia, and want guilders for my voyage:
    Therefore make present satisfaction,
    Or I 'll attach you by this officer.
Ang. Even just the sum that I do owe to you
    Is growing to me by Antipholus;
    And in the instant that I met with you
    He had of me a chain: at five o'clock   10
    I shall receive the money for the same.
    Pleaseth you walk with me down to his house,
    I will discharge my bond, and thank you too.

Enter Antipholus of Ephesus and Dromio of
    Ephesus from the courtezan's.

Off. That labor may you save: see where he comes.
Ant. E. While I go to the goldsmith's house, go
    thou
    And buy a rope's end: that will I bestow

Among my wife and her confederates,
For locking me out of my doors by day.
But, soft! I see the goldsmith. Get thee gone;
Buy thou a rope, and bring it home to me. 20

Dro. E. I buy a thousand pound a year: I buy a
  rope.   [*Exit.*

Ant. E. A man is well holp up that trusts to you:
I promised your presence and the chain;
But neither chain nor goldsmith came to me.
Belike you thought our love would last too long,
If it were chain'd together, and therefore came
  not.

Ang. Saving your merry humor, here 's the note
How much your chain weighs to the utmost
  carat,
The fineness of the gold, and chargeful fashion,
Which doth amount to three odd ducats more 30
Than I stand debted to this gentleman:
I pray you, see him presently discharged,
For he is bound to sea, and stays but for it.

Ant. E. I am not furnish'd with the present
  money;
Besides, I have some business in the town.
Good signior, take the stranger to my house,
And with you take the chain, and bid my wife
Disburse the sum on the receipt thereof:
Perchance I will be there as soon as you.

---

21. *"I buy a thousand pound a year"*; some point in these words,
familiar to Shakespeare's audience, is lost to us, and no satisfactory
explanation has as yet been given, though Halliwell's comparison of
the line with *3 Henry VI* II. ii. 144, is noteworthy:—

> "A wisp of straw were worth a thousand crowns,
> To make this shameless callet know herself."—I. G.

Ang. Then you will bring the chain to her your
self? 4

Ant. E. No; bear it with you, lest I come not time
enough.

Ang. Well, sir, I will. Have you the chain about
you?

Ant. E. An if I have not, sir, I hope you have;
Or else you may return without your money.

Ang. Nay, come, I pray you, sir, give me the
chain:

Both wind and tide stays for this gentleman,
And I, to blame, have held him here too long.

Ant. E. Good Lord! you use this dalliance to excuse

Your breach of promise to the Porpentine.
I should have chid you for not bringing it, 50
But, like a shrew, you first begin to brawl.

Sec. Mer. The hour steals on; I pray you, sir, dis-
patch.

Ang. You hear how he importunes me;—the chain!

Ant. E. Why, give it to my wife, and fetch your
money.

Ang. Come, come, you know I gave it you even
now.

Either send the chain, or send me by some
token.

Ant. E. Fie, now you run this humor out of
breath.

Come, where's the chain? I pray you, let me
see it.

Sec. Mer. My business cannot brook this dalliance.

Good sir, say whether you 'll answer me or no:
If not I 'll leave him to the officer. 61

Ant. E. I answer you! what should I answer you?

Ang. The money that you owe me for the chain.

Ant. E. I owe you none till I receive the chain.

Ang. You know I gave it you half an hour since.

Ant. E. You gave me none: you wrong me much
  to say so.

Ang. You wrong me more, sir, in denying it:
Consider how it stands upon my credit.

Sec. Mer. Well, officer, arrest him at my suit.

Off. I do; and charge you in the duke's name to
  obey me. 70

Ang. This touches me in reputation.
Either consent to pay this sum for me,
Or I attach you by this officer.

Ant. E. Consent to pay thee that I never had!
Arrest me, foolish fellow, if thou darest.

Ang. Here is thy fee; arrest him, officer.
I would not spare my brother in this case,
If he should scorn me so apparently.

Off. I do arrest you, sir: you hear the suit.

Ant. E. I do obey thee till I give thee bail. 80
But, sirrah, you shall buy this sport as dear
As all the metal in your shop will answer.

Ang. Sir, sir, I shall have law in Ephesus,
To your notorious shame; I doubt it not.

Enter Dromio of Syracuse, from the bay.

Dro. S. Master, there is a bark of Epidamnum
That stays but till her owner comes aboard,

And then, sir, she bears away. Our fraught-
age, sir,
I have convey'd aboard; and I have bought
The oil, the balsamum, and aqua-vitæ.
The ship is in her trim; the merry wind   90
Blows fair from land: they stay for nought at
all
But for their owner, master, and yourself.

Ant. E. How now! a madman! Why, thou peevish sheep,
What ship of Epidamnum stays for me?

Dro. S. A ship you sent me to, to hire waftage.

Ant. E. Thou drunken slave, I sent thee for a
rope,
And told thee to what purpose and what end.

Dro. S. You sent me for a rope's end as soon:
You sent me to the bay, sir, for a bark.

Ant. E. I will debate this matter at more leisure.
And teach your ears to list me with more
heed.   101
To Adriana, villain, hie thee straight:
Give her this key, and tell her, in the desk
That 's cover'd o'er with Turkish tapestry
There is a purse of ducats; let her send it:
Tell her I am arrested in the street,
And that shall bail me: hie thee, slave, be gone!
On, officer, to prison till it come.

       [*Exeunt Sec. Merchant, Angelo, Officer,*
                              and Ant. E.

Dro. S. To Adriana! that is where we dined,
Where Dowsabel did claim me for her husband: 110

She is too big, I hope, for me to compass.
Thither I must, although against my will,
For servants must their masters' minds fulfill.
[*Exit.*

SCENE II

The house of Antipholus of Ephesus.

Enter Adriana and Luciana.

Adr. Ah, Luciana, did he tempt thee so?
Mightst thou perceive austerely in his eye
That he did plead in earnest? yea or no?
Look'd he or red or pale, or sad or merrily?
What observation madest thou, in this case,
Of his heart's meteors tilting in his face?

Luc. First he denied you had in him no right.

Adr. He meant he did me none; the more my spite.

Luc. Then swore he that he was a stranger here.

Adr. And true he swore, though yet forsworn he
were.   10

Luc. Then pleaded I for you.

Adr.   And what said he?

Luc. That love I begg'd for you he begg'd of me.

Adr. With what persuasion did he tempt thy love?

6. The allusion is to those meteors which have sometimes been
thought to resemble armies meeting in the shock of battle. The
following in the second book of *Paradise Lost* best explains it:

> "As when, to warn proud cities, war appears,
> Wag'd in the troubled sky, and armies rush
> To battle in the clouds, before each van
> Prick forth the aery knights, and couch their spears,
> Till thickest legions close; with feats of arms
> From either end of heaven the welkin burns."—H. N. H.

Luc. With words that in an honest suit might move,
　　First he did praise my beauty, then my speech.
Adr. Didst speak him fair?
Luc.　　　　　　　　Have patience, I beseech.
Adr. I cannot, nor I will not, hold me still;
　　My tongue, though not my heart, shall have his
　　　　will.
　　He is deformed, crooked, old, and sere,
　　Ill-faced, worse bodied, shapeless everywhere;
　　Vicious, ungentle, foolish, blunt, unkind;　　21
　　Stigmatical in making, worse in mind.
Luc. Who would be jealous, then, of such a one?
　　No evil lost is wail'd when it is gone.
Adr. Ah, but I think him better than I say,
　　And yet would herein others' eyes were worse.
　　Far from her nest the lapwing cries away:
　　My heart prays for him, though my tongue
　　　　do curse.

Enter Dromio of Syracuse.

Dro. S. Here! go; the desk, the purse! sweet, now,
　　make haste.
Luc. How hast thou lost thy breath?
Dro. S.　　　　　　　　By running fast.　　30
Adr. Where is thy master, Dromio? is he well?
Dro. S. No, he 's in Tartar limbo, worse than hell.
　　A devil in an everlasting garment hath him;
　　One whose hard heart is button'd up with steel;
　　A fiend, a fury, pitiless and rough;

35. *"A fiend, a fury";* the Folios read *"fairy,"* corrected by Theobald, who has been followed by most editors, including the Cambridge editors; a strong case can, however, be made for the original
reading.—I. G.

A wolf, nay, worse; a fellow all in buff;
A back-friend, a shoulder-clapper, one that
    countermands
The passages of alleys, creeks, and narrow
    lands;
A hound that runs counter, and yet draws dry-
    foot well:
One that, before the Judgment, carries poor
    souls to hell.   40

Adr. Why, man, what is the matter?

Dro. S. I do not know the matter: he is 'rested on
    the case.

Adr. What, is he arrested? Tell me at whose suit.

Dro. S. I know not at whose suit he is arrested
    well;
But he's in a suit of buff which 'rested him, that
    can I tell.
Will you send him, mistress, redemption, the
    money in his desk?

Adr. Go fetch it, sister. [*Exit Luciana.*] This I
    wonder at,
That he, unknown to me, should be in debt.
Tell me, was he arrested on a band?

Dro. S. Not on a band, but on a stronger thing; 50
A chain, a chain! Do you not hear it ring?

Adr. What, the chain?

Dro. S. No, no, the bell: 'tis time that I were gone:

---

40. *"Hell"* was the cant term for prison. There was a place of
this name under the Exchequer, where the king's debtors were con-
fined.—H. N. H.

49. *"Band,"* that is *bond.* Shakespeare takes advantage of the
old spelling to produce a quibble.—H. N. H.

It was two ere I left him, and now the clock
strikes one.

Adr. The hours come back! that did I never hear.

Dro. S. O, yes; if any hour meet a sergeant, 'a
turns back for very fear.

Adr. As if Time were in debt! how fondly dost
thou reason!

Dro. S. Time is a very bankrupt, and owes more
than he's worth to season.

Nay, he's a thief too: have you not heard men
say,

That Time comes stealing on by night and day?

If Time be in debt and theft, and a sergeant in
the way, 61

Hath he not reason to turn back an hour in a
day?

Re-enter Luciana with a purse.

Adr. Go, Dromio; there's the money, bear it
straight;

And bring thy master home immediately.

Come, sister: I am press'd down with conceit,—

Conceit, my comfort and my injury.

[*Exeunt.*

---

61. *"If Time be in debt";* the Folios read *"If I,"* where *I* is probably an error for *'a* (*i. e. he*) or *he;* the reading in the text is
Rowe's emendation.—I. G.

SCENE III

A public place.

Enter Antipholus of Syracuse.

Ant. S. There 's not a man I meet but doth salute
  me
  As if I were their well-acquainted friend:
  And every one doth call me by my name.
  Some tender money to me; some invite me;
  Some other give me thanks for kindnesses;
  Some offer me commodities to buy:
  Even now a tailor call'd me in his shop,
  And show'd me silks that he had bought for me,
  And therewithal took measure of my body.
  Sure, these are but imaginary wiles,   10
  And Lapland sorcerers inhabit here.

Enter Dromio of Syracuse.

Dro. S. Master, here 's the gold you sent me
  for.   What, have you got the picture of old
  Adam new-apparelled?

Ant. S. What gold is this? what Adam dost thou
  mean?

Dro. S. Not that Adam that kept the Paradise,

11. *"Lapland sorcerers."* Lapland was the subject of much Elizabethan legend. Fletcher in *The Chances* relates that they there "sell men winds for dead drinks and old doublets"; Milton refers to "Lapland witches," Marlowe to "Lapland giants."—C. H. H.

13. *"What, have you got the picture of old Adam new-apparelled?"* *"The picture of old Adam"*= the sergeant, who was clad *"in buff"*; in Elizabethan slang this latter phrase was used in the sense of

but that Adam that keeps the prison: he that
goes in the calf's skin that was killed for the
Prodigal; he that came behind you, sir, like
an evil angel, and bid you forsake your lib-   20
erty.

Ant. S. I understand thee not.

Dro. S. No? why, 'tis a plain case: he that went
like a base-viol, in a case of leather; the man,
sir, that, when gentlemen are tired, gives
them a sob and 'rests them; he, sir, that takes
pity on decayed men, and gives them suits of
durance; he that sets up his rest to do more
exploits with his mace than a morris-pike.

Ant. S. What, thou meanest an officer?   30

Dro. S. Aye, sir, the sergeant of the band; he
that brings any man to answer it that breaks
his band; one that thinks a man always going to bed, and says, 'God give you good
rest!'

Ant. S. Well, sir, there rest in your foolery.
Is there any ship puts forth to-night? may
we be gone?

Dro. S. Why, sir, I brought you word an hour
since, that the bark Expedition put forth to-   40

"bare skin," *i. e.* "naked"; hence the quibble. *New-apparelled* offers
some difficulty, and depends on the general construction of the whole
line. It has been ingeniously suggested that the idea is "got him a
new *suit*," *i. e.* "got rid of him." On the other hand, there is a possibility that the phrase *"What have you got?"* is a vulgarism for
"What have you done with?" Theobald proposed to read *"What,
have you got rid of the picture,"* &c. In the latter cases *new-
apparelled* must be regarded as merely a descriptive epithet, the
whole phrase *"the picture of old Adam new-apparelled"* being an
elaborate circumlocution for "sergeant."—I. G.

night; and then were you hindered by the sergeant, to tarry for the hoy Delay.   Here
are the angels that you sent for to deliver
you.

Ant. S. The fellow is distract, and so am I;
And here we wander in illusions:
Some blessed power deliver us from hence!

Enter a Courtezan.

Cour. Well met, well met, Master Antipholus,
I see, sir, you have found the goldsmith now:
Is that the chain you promised me to-day?   50

Ant. S. Satan, avoid! I charge thee, tempt me not.

Dro. S. Master, is this Mistress Satan?

Ant. S. It is the devil.

Dro. S. Nay, she is worse, she is the devil's dam;
and here she comes in the habit of a light
wench: and thereof comes that the wenches
say, 'God damn me;' that 's as much to say,
'God make me a light wench.'   It is written, they appear to men like angels of light:
light is an effect of fire, and fire will burn: 60
ergo, light wenches will burn.   Come not
near her.

Cour. Your man and you are marvellous merry, sir.
Will you go with me?   We 'll mend our dinner
here?

Dro. S. Master, if you do, expect spoon-meat;
or bespeak a long spoon.

Ant. S. Why, Dromio?

64. *"We'll mend our dinner,"* i. e. "we'll buy something more for
our dinner."—I. G.

Dro. S. Marry, he must have a long spoon that
must eat with the devil.

Ant. S. Avoid then, fiend! what tell'st thou me of
supping? 7(

Thou art, as you are all, a sorceress:

I conjure thee to leave me and be gone.

Cour. Give me the ring of mine you had at dinner,

Or, for my diamond, the chain you promised,

And I 'll be gone, sir, and not trouble you.

Dro. S. Some devils ask but the parings of one's
nail,

A rush, a hair, a drop of blood, a pin,

A nut, a cherry-stone;

But she, more covetous, would have a chain.

Master, be wise: and if you give it her, 8(

The devil will shake her chain, and fright us
with it.

Cour. I pray you, sir, my ring, or else the chain:

I hope you do not mean to cheat me so.

Ant. S. Avaunt, thou witch! Come, Dromio, let
us go.

Dro. S. 'Fly pride,' says the peacock: mistress
that you know. [*Exeunt Ant. S. and Dro. S*

Cour. Now, out of doubt Antipholus is mad,

Else would he never so demean himself.

A ring he hath of mine worth forty ducats,

And for the same he promised me a chain:

Both one and other he denies me now. 9(

77. *"a drop of blood"*; probably an allusion to Faustus' signa-
ture of the bond in his blood. Marlowe's *Dr. Faustus* had been
written a year or more before this Comedy, and the English version
of the *Faustbuch* (reprinted 1592) may also already have appeared
—C. H. H.

The reason that I gather he is mad,
Besides this present instance of his rage,
Is a mad tale he told to-day at dinner,
Of his own doors being shut against his en-
    trance.
Belike his wife, acquainted with his fits,
On purpose shut the doors against his way.
My way is now to hie home to his house,
And tell his wife that, being lunatic,
He rush'd into my house, and took perforce 99
My ring away.   This course I fittest choose;
For forty ducats is too much to lose.   [*Exit.*

SCENE IV

A street.

Enter Antipholus of Ephesus and the Officer.

Ant. E. Fear me not, man; I will not break away:
I 'll give thee, ere I leave thee, so much money,
To warrant thee, as I am 'rested for.
My wife is in a wayward mood to-day,
And will not lightly trust the messenger.
That I should be attach'd in Ephesus,
I tell you, 'twill sound harshly in her ears.

Enter Dromio of Ephesus with a rope's-end.

Here comes my man; I think he brings the
    money.
How now, sir! have you that I sent you for?

Dro. E. Here's that, I warrant you, will pay them
    all.

Ant. E. But where's the money?

Dro. E. Why, sir, I gave the money for the rope.

Ant. E. Five hundred ducats, villain, for a rope?

Dro. E. I'll serve you, sir, five hundred at the rate.

Ant. E. To what end did I bid thee hie thee home?

Dro. E. To a rope's-end, sir; and to that end
    am I returned.

Ant. E. And to that end, sir, I will welcome you.
                              [Beating him.

Off. Good sir, be patient.

Dro. E. Nay, 'tis for me to be patient: I am in   20
    adversity.

Off. Good now, hold thy tongue.

Dro. E. Nay, rather persuade him to hold his
    hands.

Ant. E. Thou whoreson, senseless villain!

Dro. E. I would I were senseless, sir, that I
    might not feel your blows.

Ant. E. Thou are sensible in nothing but blows,
    and so is an ass.

Dro. E. I am an ass, indeed; you may prove it   30
    by my long ears. I have served him from
    the hour of my nativity to this instant, and
    have nothing at his hands for my service
    but blows. When I am cold, he heats me
    with beating; when I am warm, he cools
    me with beating: I am waked with it when
    I sleep; raised with it when I sit; driven
    out of doors with it when I go from home;
    welcomed home with it when I return: nay,

I bear it on my shoulders, as a beggar wont 40
   her brat; and, I think, when he hath lamed
   me, I shall beg with it from door to door.

Ant. E. Come, go along; my wife is coming
   yonder.

Enter Adriana, Luciana, the Courtezan, and Pinch.

Dro. E. Mistress, 'respice finem,' respect your
   end; or rather, the prophecy like the parrot, 'beware the rope's-end.'

Ant. E. Wilt thou still talk?   [*Beating him.*

Cour. How say you now? is not your husband
   mad?   50

Adr. His incivility confirms no less.
   Good Doctor Pinch, you are a conjurer;
   Establish him in his true sense again,
   And I will please you what you will demand.

Luc. Alas, how fiery and how sharp he looks!

Cour. Mark how he trembles in his ecstasy!

---

46. *"The prophecy like the parrot, beware the rope's-end";* the
Cambridge editors most ingeniously conjecture that we should read:—

        "or, rather, 'prospice funem,' beware the rope's-end.
Antipholus of E. Wilt thou still talk like the parrot?"

Dyce proposed, *"or, rather, to prophecy, like,"* &c.
Parrots were taught uncomplimentary remarks in Elizabethan
times, as they are at present; there are many allusions to the very
phrase in the text: Ralpho, in Butler's Hudibras,

     "Could tell what subtlest parrots mean,
       That speak, but think contrary clean;
       What member 't is of whom they talk,
       When they cry rope, and walk, knave, walk."—I. G.

56. This *tremor* was anciently thought to be a sure indication of
being possessed by the devil. Caliban in *The Tempest* says—"Thou
dost me yet but little hurt; thou wilt anon, I know it by thy *trem-
bling.*"—H. N. H.

Pinch. Give me your hand, and let me feel your
     pulse.

Ant. E. There is my hand, and let it feel your
     ear.   [*Striking him.*

Pinch. I charge thee, Satan, housed within this
     man,   60

To yield possession to my holy prayers,

And to thy state of darkness hie thee straight:

I conjure thee by all the saints in heaven!

Ant. E. Peace, doting wizard, peace! I am not
     mad.

Adr. O, that thou wert not, poor distressed soul!

Ant. E. You minion, you, are these your custom-
     ers?

Did this companion with the saffron face

Revel and feast it at my house to-day,

Whilst upon me the guilty doors were shut,

And I denied to enter in my house?   70

Adr. O husband, God doth know you dined at
     home;

Where would you had remain'd until this time,

Free from these slanders and this open shame!

Ant. E. Dined at home! Thou villain, what say-
     est thou?

Dro. E. Sir, sooth to say, you did not dine at home.

Ant. E. Were not my doors lock'd up, and I shut
     out?

Dro. E. Perdie, your doors were lock'd, and you
     shut out.

Ant. E. And did not she herself revile me there?

Dro. E. Sans fable, she herself reviled you there.

Ant. E. Did not her kitchen-maid, rail, taunt, and
    scorn me?   80
Dro. E. Certes, she did; the kitchen-vestal scorned
    you.
Ant. E. And did not I in rage depart from
    thence?
Dro. E. In verity you did; my bones bear wit-
    ness,
    That since have felt the vigor of his rage.
Adr. Is 't good to soothe him in these contraries?
Pinch. It is no shame: the fellow finds his vein,
    And, yielding to him, humors well his frenzy.
Ant. E. Thou hast suborn'd the goldsmith to ar-
    rest me.
Adr. Alas, I sent you money to redeem you,   89
    By Dromio here, who have came in haste for it.
Dro. E. Money by me! heart and good-will you
    might;
    But surely, master, not a rag of money.
Ant. E. Went'st not thou to her for a purse of du-
    cats?
Adr. He came to me, and I deliver'd it.
Luc. And I am witness with her that she did.
Dro. E. God and the rope-maker bear me witness
    That I was sent for nothing but a rope!
Pinch. Mistress, both man and master is possess'd;
    I know it by their pale and deadly looks:
    They must be bound, and laid in some dark
    room.   100
Ant. E. Say, wherefore didst thou lock me forth
    to-day?
    And why dost thou deny the bag of gold?

Adr. I did not, gentle husband, lock thee forth.

Dro. E. And, gentle master, I received no gold;
But I confess, sir, that we were lock'd out.

Adr. Dissembling villain, thou speak'st false in
both.

Ant. E. Dissembling harlot, thou art false in all;
And art confederate with a damned pack
To make a loathsome abject scorn of me:
But with these nails I'll pluck out these false
eyes,   110
That would behold in me this shameful sport.

*Enter three or four, and offer to bind him. He
strives.*

Adr. O, bind him, bind him! let him not come near
me.

Pinch. More company! The fiend is strong within him.

Luc. Aye me, poor man, how pale and wan he
looks!

Ant. E. What, will you murder me? Thou jailer,
thou,
I am thy prisoner: wilt thou suffer them
To make a rescue?

Off.   Masters, let him go:
He is my prisoner, and you shall not have him.

Pinch. Go bind this man, for he is frantic too.
                              [*They offer to bind Dro. E.*

Adr. What wilt thou do, thou peevish officer? 120
Hast thou delight to see a wretched man
Do outrage and displeasure to himself?

Off. He is my prisoner: if I let him go,

66

The debt he owes will be required of me.

Adr. I will discharge thee ere I go from thee:
Bear me forthwith unto his creditor,
And, knowing how the debt grows, I will pay it.
Good master doctor, see him safe convey'd
Home to my house.   O most unhappy day!

Ant. E. O most unhappy strumpet!   130

Dro. E. Master, I am here enter'd in bond for
you.

Ant. E. Out on thee, villain! wherefore dost thou
mad me?

Dro. E. Will you be bound for nothing? be mad,
good master: cry, The devil!

Luc. God help, poor souls, how idly do they talk!

Adr. Go bear him hence.   Sister, go you with me.
[*Exeunt all but Adriana, Luciana, Officer
and Courtezan.*

Say now; whose suit is he arrested at?

Off. One Angelo, a goldsmith: do you know him?

Adr. I know the man.   What is the sum he owes?

Off. Two hundred ducats.

Adr.   Say, how grows it due?

Off. Due for a chain your husband had of him. 141

Adr. He did bespeak a chain for me, but had it
not.

Cour. When as your husband, all in rage, to-day
Came to my house, and took away my ring—
The ring I saw upon his finger now,—
Straight after did I meet him with a chain.

Adr. It may be so, but I did never see it.
Come, jailer, bring me where the goldsmith is:
I long to know the truth hereof at large.

*Enter Antipholus of Syracuse with his rapier
drawn, and Dromio of Syracuse.*

Luc. God, for thy mercy! they are loose again.
Adr. And come with naked swords.　　　　151
　　　Let's call more help to have them bound again.
Off. Away! they'll kill us.
　　　　　　[Exeunt all but Ant. S. and Dro. S.
Ant. S. I see these witches are afraid of swords.
Dro. S. She that would be your wife now ran from
　　　you.
Ant. S. Come to the Centaur; fetch our stuff
　　　from thence:
　　　I long that we were safe and sound aboard.
Dro. S. Faith, stay here this night; they will
　　　surely do us no harm: you saw they speak
　　　us fair, give us gold: methinks they are 160
　　　such a gentle nation, that, but for the
　　　mountain of mad flesh that claims mar-
　　　riage of me, I could find in my heart to stay
　　　here still, and turn witch.
Ant. S. I will not stay to-night for all the
　　　town;
　　　Therefore away, to get our stuff aboard.
　　　　　　　　　　　　　　[Exeunt.

ACT FIFTH

SCENE I

A street before a Priory.

Enter Second Merchant and Angelo.

Ang. I am sorry, sir, that I have hinder'd you;
    But, I protest, he had the chain of me,
    Though most dishonestly he doth deny it.
Sec. Mer. How is the man esteem'd here in the
    city?
Ang. Of very reverent reputation, sir,
    Of credit infinite, highly beloved,
    Second to none that lives here in the city:
    His word might bear my wealth at any time.
Sec. Mer. Speak softly: yonder, as I think, he
    walks.

*Enter Antipholus of Syracuse and Dromio of
Syracuse.*

Ang. 'Tis so; and that self chain about his neck, 10
    Which he forswore most monstrously to have.
    Good sir, draw near to me, I 'll speak to him;
    Signior Antipholus, I wonder much
    That you would put me to this shame and trou-
    ble;
    And, not without some scandal to yourself,

With circumstance and oath so to deny
This chain which now you wear so openly:
Beside the charge, the shame, imprisonment,
You have done wrong to this my honest friend;
Who, but for staying on our controversy,   20
Had hoisted sail and put to sea to-day:
This chain you had of me; can you deny it?

Ant. S. I think I had; I never did deny it.

Sec. Mer. Yes, that you did, sir, and forswore it
  too.

Ant. S. Who heard me to deny it or forswear it?

Sec. Mer. These ears of mine, thou know'st, did
  hear thee.
  Fie on thee, wretch! 'tis pity that thou livest
  To walk where any honest men resort.

Ant. S. Thou art a villain to impeach me thus:
  I'll prove mine honor and mine honesty,   30
  Against thee presently, if thou darest stand.

Sec. Mer. I dare, and do defy thee for a villain.
                    [*They draw.*

*Enter Adriana, Luciana, the Courtezan, and
  others.*

Adr. Hold, hurt him not, for God's sake! he is
  mad.
  Some get within him, take his sword away:
  Bind Dromio too, and bear them to my house.

Dro. S. Run, master, run; for God's sake, take a
  house!
  This is some priory. In, or we are spoil'd!
                    [*Exeunt Ant. S. and Dro. S. to the Priory.*

Enter the Lady Abbess.

Abb. Be quiet, people. Wherefore throng you
  hither?

Adr. To fetch my poor distracted husband hence.
  Let us come in, that we may bind him fast, 40
  And bear him home for his recovery.

Ang. I knew he was not in his perfect wits.

Sec. Mer. I am sorry now that I did draw on him.

Abb. How long hath this possession held the man?

Adr. This week he hath been heavy, sour, sad,
  And much different from the man he was;
  But till this afternoon his passion
  Ne'er brake into extremity of rage.

Abb. Hath he not lost much wealth by wreck of
  sea?
  Buried some dear friend? Hath not else his
  eye   50
  Stray'd his affection in unlawful love?
  A sin prevailing much in youthful men,
  Who give their eyes the liberty of gazing.
  Which of these sorrows is he subject to?

Adr. To none of these, except it be the last;
  Namely, some love that drew him oft from
  home.

Abb. You should for that have reprehended him.

Adr. Why, so I did.

Abb.   Aye, but not rough enough.

Adr. As roughly as my modesty would let me.

---

46. *"And much different,"* &c., the second Folio, for the sake of
the meter, reads *much much;* a reading which does ᵔot ᵔommend
itself; *too much* has been conjectured. The line as ıt stands is certainly doubtful; *different* does not occur in Shakespeare.—I. G.

Abb. Haply, in private.

Adr.   And in assemblies too.   60

Abb. Aye, but not enough.

Adr. It was the copy of our conference:

    In bed, he slept not for my urging it;

    At board, he fed not for my urging it;

    Alone, it was the subject of my theme;

    In company I often glanced it;

    Still did I tell him it was vile and bad.

Abb. And thereof came it that the man was mad.

    The venom clamors of a jealous woman

    Poisons more deadly than a mad dog's tooth. 70

    It seems his sleeps were hinder'd by thy railing:

    And thereof comes it that his head is light.

    Thou say'st his meat was sauced with thy up-

        braidings:

    Unquiet meals make ill digestions;

    Thereof the raging fire of fever bred;

    And what's a fever but a fit of madness?

    Thou say'st his sports were hinder'd by thy

        brawls:

    Sweet recreation barr'd, what doth ensue

    But moody and dull melancholy,

    Kinsman to grim and comfortless despair; 80

    And at her heels a huge infectious troop

66. *"Glancéd it";* Pope's conjectural *at it* is unnecessary, though *glance* in the sense *to hint,* used transitively, does not otherwise occur; Folio 1 does not elide the *ed* of *glanced.*—I. G.

79. *"But moody and dull melancholy";* something is obviously amiss with the line; *moody moping* has been suggested. *Kinsman* in the next line is used in its general sense of *akin,* which some editors have unnecessarily substituted; it has even been changed to *kins-woman.*—I. G.

81. This *"her,"* referring to *kinsman,* seems to have puzzled the

Of pale distemperatures and foes to life?
In food, in sport, and life-preserving rest
To be disturb'd, would mad or man or beast:
The consequence is, then, thy jealous fits
Have scared thy husband from the use of wits.
Luc. She never reprehended him but mildly,
When he demean'd himself rough, rude, and
wildly.
Why bear you these rebukes, and answer not?
Adr. She did betray me to my own reproof.   90
Good people, enter, and lay hold on him.
Abb. No, not a creature enters in my house.
Adr. Then let your servants bring my husband
forth.
Abb. Neither: he took this place for sanctuary,
And it shall privilege him from your hands
Till I have brought him to his wits again,
Or lose my labor in assaying it.
Adr. I will attend my husband, be his nurse,
Diet his sickness, for it is my office,
And will have no attorney but myself;   100
And therefore let me have him home with me.
Abb. Be patient; for I will not let him stir
Till I have used the approved means I have,
With wholesome syrups, drugs and holy pray-
ers,
To make of him a formal man again:
It is a branch and parcel of mine oath,

commentators. It was no very wonderful thing for such words to
be applied to females. Thus in *The Merchant of Venice* Portia
says,—"But now I was the *lord* of this fair mansion, *master* of my
servants."—H. N. H.

A charitable duty of my order.

Therefore depart, and leave him here with me.

Adr. I will not hence, and leave my husband here:

And ill it doth beseem your holiness   110

To separate the husband and the wife.

Abb. Be quiet, and depart: thou shalt not have

him.   [*Exit.*

Luc. Complain unto the Duke of this indignity.

Adr. Come, go: I will fall prostrate at his feet,

And never rise until my tears and prayers

Have won his Grace to come in person hither,

And take perforce my husband from the ab-

bess.

Sec. Mer. By this, I think, the dial points at five:

Anon, I 'm sure, the Duke himself in person

Comes this way to the melancholy vale,   120

The place of death and sorry execution,

Behind the ditches of the abbey here.

Ang. Upon what cause?

Sec. Mer. To see a reverend Syracusian merchant,

Who put unluckily into this bay

Against the laws and statutes of this town,

Beheaded publicly for his offense.

Ang. See where they come: we will behold his

death.

Luc. Kneel to the Duke before he pass the abbey.

*Enter Duke, attended; Ægeon bareheaded; with
the Headsman and other Officers.*

Duke. Yet once again proclaim it publicly,   130

If any friend will pay the sum for him,

He shall not die; so much we tender him.

Adr. Justice, most sacred Duke, against the abbess!

Duke. She is a virtuous and a reverend lady:

It cannot be that she hath done thee wrong.

Adr. May it please your grace, Antipholus my husband,—

Whom I made lord of me and all I had,

At your important letters,—this ill day

A most outrageous fit of madness took him;

That desperately he hurried through the street,—   140

With him his bondman, all as mad as he,—

Doing displeasure to the citizens

By rushing in their houses, bearing thence

Rings, jewels, any thing his rage did like.

Once did I get him bound, and sent him home,

Whilst to take order for the wrongs I went,

That here and there his fury had committed.

Anon, I wot not by what strong escape,

He broke from those that had the guard of him;

And with his mad attendant and himself,   150

Each one with ireful passion, with drawn swords,

Met us again, and, madly went on us,

Chased us away; till, raising of more aid,

We came again to bind them. Then they fled

Into this abbey, whither we pursued them;

And here the abbess shuts the gates on us,

And will not suffer us to fetch him out,

Nor send him forth, that we may bear him hence.

Therefore, most gracious Duke, with thy com-
    mand
Let him be brought forth, and borne hence for
    help. 160

Duke. Long since thy husband served me in my
    wars;
And I to thee engaged a prince's word,
When thou didst make him master of thy bed,
To do him all the grace and good I could.
Go, some of you, knock at the abbey-gate,
And bid the lady abbess come to me.
I will determine this before I stir.

Enter a Servant.

Serv. O mistress, mistress, shift and save yourself!
My master and his man are both broke loose,
Beaten the maids a-row, and bound the doc-
    tor, 170
Whose beard they have singed off with brands
    of fire;
And ever, as it blazed, they threw on him
Great pails of puddled mire to quench the hair:
My master preaches patience to him, and the
    while
His man with scissors nicks him like a fool;

170. *"Beaten the maids,"* &c., *i. e. have beaten;* but the previous
verb has *are,*—a confusion of constructions which causes little difficulty, and fairly common in Elizabethan English.—I. G.

175. The heads of fools were shaved, or their hair cut close, as
appears by the following passage in *The Choice of Change,* 1598.
"Three things used by monks which provoke other men to laugh
at their follies. 1. They are *shaven* and *notched* on the head *like
fooles."* Florio explains, *"zuccone,* a shaven pate, a notted poll, a
poll-pate, a gull, a *ninnie."*—H. N. H.

And sure, unless you send some present help,
Between them they will kill the conjurer.

Adr. Peace, fool! thy master and his man are here;
And that is false thou dost report to us.

Serv. Mistress, upon my life, I tell you true;   180
I have not breathed almost since I did see it.
He cries for you, and vows, if he can take you,
To scorch your face and to disfigure you.

                        [*Cry within.*

Hark, hark! I hear him, mistress: fly, be gone!

Duke. Come, stand by me; fear nothing.   Guard
    with halberds!

Adr. Aye me, it is my husband!   Witness you,
That he is borne about invisible:
Even now we housed him in the abbey here;
And now he 's there, past thought of human
    reason.

*Enter Antipholus of Ephesus and Dromio of
                Ephesus.*

Ant. E. Justice, most gracious Duke, O, grant
    me justice!   190
Even for the service that long since I did thee,
When I bestrid thee in the wars, and took
Deep scars to save thy life; even for the blood
That then I lost for thee, now grant me justice.

Æge. Unless the fear of death doth make me
    dote,
I see my son Antipholus, and Dromio.

Ant. E. Justice, sweet prince, against that woman
    there!
She whom thou gavest to me to be my wife,

That hath abused and dishonor'd me
Even in the strength and height of injury: 200
Beyond imagination is the wrong
That she this day hath shameless thrown on me

Duke. Discover how, and thou shalt find me just

Ant. E. This day, great Duke, she shut the doors
  upon me,
While she with harlots feasted in my house.

Duke. A grievous fault! Say, woman, didst thou
  so?

Adr. No, my good lord: myself, he and my sister
To-day did dine together. So befall my soul
As this is false he burthens me withal!

Luc. Ne'er may I look on day, nor sleep on night
But she tells to your highness simple truth! 211

Ang. O perjured woman! They are both forsworn:
In this the madman justly chargeth them.

Ant. E. My liege, I am advised what I say;
Neither disturbed with the effect of wine,
Nor heady-rash, provoked with raging ire,
Albeit my wrongs might make one wiser mad.
This woman lock'd me out this day from dinner:
That goldsmith there, were he not pack'd with
  her,
Could witness it, for he was with me then; 220
Who parted with me to go fetch a chain,
Promising to bring it to the Porpentine,
Where Balthazar and I did dine together.
Our dinner done, and he not coming thither,

---

205. *"Harlot"* was a term anciently applied to a rogue or base person among men, as well as to wantons among women.—H. N. H.

I went to seek him: in the street I met him,
And in his company that gentleman.
There did this perjured goldsmith swear me
    down
That I this day of him received the chain,
Which, God he knows, I saw not: for the
    which
He did arrest me with an officer.   230
I did obey; and sent my peasant home
For certain ducats: he with none return'd.
Then fairly I bespoke the officer
To go in person with me to my house.
By the way we met my wife, her sister, and a
    rabble more
Of vile confederates. Along with them
They brought one Pinch, a hungry lean-faced
    villain,
A mere anatomy, a mountebank,
A threadbare juggler, and a fortune-teller,
A needy, hollow-eyed, sharp-looking wretch,
A living dead man: this pernicious slave,   241
Forsooth, took on him as a conjurer;
And, gazing in mine eyes, feeling my pulse,
And with no face, as 'twere, outfacing me,
Cries out, I was possess'd. Then all together
They fell upon me, bound me, bore me thence,
And in a dark and dankish vault at home
There left me and my man, both bound to-
    gether;
Till, gnawing with my teeth my bonds in sun-
    der,
I gain'd my freedom, and immediately   250

Ran hither to your Grace; whom I beseech
To give me ample satisfaction
For these deep shames and great indignities.

Ang. My lord, in truth, thus far I witness with
him,
That he dined not at home, but was lock'd out.

Duke. But had he such a chain of thee or no?

Ang. He had, my lord: and when he ran in here,
These people saw the chain about his neck.

Sec. Mer. Besides, I will be sworn these ears of
mine
Heard you confess you had the chain of him,
After you first forswore it on the mart: 261
And thereupon I drew my sword on you;
And then you fled into this abbey here,
From whence, I think, you are come by mira-
cle.

Ant. E. I never came within these abbey-walls;
Nor ever didst thou draw thy sword on me:
I never saw the chain, so help me Heaven!
And this is false you burthen me withal.

Duke. Why, what an intricate impeach is this!
I think you all have drunk of Circe's cup. 270
If here you housed him, here he would have
been;
If he were mad, he would not plead so coldly:
You say he dined at home; the goldsmith here
Denies that saying. Sirrah, what say you?

Dro. E. Sir, he dined with her there, at the Porpentine.

Cour. He did; and from my finger snatch'd that
ring.

80

Ant. E. 'Tis true, my liege; this ring I had of her.

Duke. Saw'st thou him enter at the abbey here?

Cour. As sure, my liege, as I do see your Grace.

Duke. Why, this is strange.   Go call the abbess
    hither.   280
    I think you are all mated, or stark mad.

                          [Exit one to the Abbess.

Æge. Most mighty Duke, vouchsafe me speak **a**
    word:
    Haply I see a friend will save my life,
    And pay the sum that may deliver me.

Duke. Speak freely, Syracusian, what thou wilt.

Æge. Is not your name, sir, call'd Antipholus?
    And is not that your bondman, Dromio?

Dro. E. Within this hour I was his bondman, sir,
    But he, I thank him, gnaw'd in two my cords:
    Now am I Dromio, and his man unbound.   290

Æge. I am sure you both of you remember me.

Dro. E. Ourselves we do remember, sir, by you;
    For lately we were bound, as you are now.
    You are not Pinch's patient, are you, sir?

Æge. Why look you strange on me? you know me
    well.

Ant. E. I never saw you in my life till now.

Æge. O, grief hath changed me since you saw me
    last,
    And careful hours with time's deformed hand
    Have written strange defeatures in my face:
    But tell me yet, dost thou not know my voice?

Ant. E. Neither.   301

Æge. Dromio, nor thou?

Dro. E.   No, trust me, sir, nor I.

Æge. I am sure thou dost.

Dro. E. Aye, sir, but I am sure I do not; and
whatsoever a man denies, you are now
bound to believe him.

Æge. Not know my voice! O time's extremity,
Hast thou so crack'd and splitted my poor
tongue
In seven short years, that here my only son
Knows not my feeble key of untuned cares? 310
Though now this grained face of mine be hid
In sap-consuming winter's drizzled snow,
And all the conduits of my blood froze up,
Yet hath my night of life some memory,
My wasting lamps some fading glimmer left,
My dull deaf ears a little use to hear:
All these old witnesses—I cannot err—
Tell me thou art my son Antipholus.

Ant. E. I never saw my father in my life.

Æge. But seven years since, in Syracusa, boy, 320
Thou know'st we parted: but perhaps, my son,
Thou shamest to acknowledge me in misery.

Ant. E. The Duke and all that know me in the
city
Can witness with me that it is not so:
I ne'er saw Syracusa in my life.

Duke. I tell thee, Syracusian, twenty years
Have I been patron to Antipholus,
During which time he ne'er saw Syracusa:
I see thy age and dangers make thee dote.

310. *"My feeble key of untuned cares"; i. e.* "the feeble tone of my
voice, which gives utterance to nothing but unharmonious grief."—
I. G.

*Re-enter Abbess, with Antipholus of Syracuse and
Dromio of Syracuse.*

Abb. Most mighty Duke, behold a man much
    wrong'd.   *[All gather to see them.*

Adr. I see two husbands, or mine eyes deceive
    me.   331

Duke. One of these men is Genius to the other;
    And so of these.   Which is the natural man,
    And which the spirit? who deciphers them?

Dro. S. I, sir, am Dromio: command him away.

Dro. E. I, sir, am Dromio; pray, let me stay.

Ant. S. Ægeon art thou not? or else his ghost?

Dro. S. O, my old master! who hath bound him
    here?

Abb. Whoever bound him, I will loose his bonds,
    And gain a husband by his liberty.   340
    Speak, old Ægeon, if thou be'st the man
    That hadst a wife once call'd Æmilia,
    That bore thee at a burthen two fair sons:
    O, if thou be'st the same Ægeon, speak,
    And speak unto the same Æmilia!

Æge. If I dream not, thou art Æmilia:
    If thou art she, tell me, where is that son
    That floated with thee on the fatal raft?

Abb. By men of Epidamnum he and I
    And the twin Dromio, all were taken up;   350
    But by and by rude fishermen of Corinth
    By force took Dromio and my son from them,
    And me they left with those of Epidamnum.
    What then became of them I cannot tell;
    I to this fortune that you see me in.

Duke. Why, here begins his morning story right:
These two Antipholuses, these two so like,
And these two Dromios, one in semblance,—
Besides her urging of her wreck at sea,—
These are the parents to these children,   360
Which accidentally are met together.
Antipholus, thou camest from Corinth first?

Ant. S. No, sir, not I; I came from Syracuse.

Duke. Stay, stand apart; I know not which is
which.

Ant. E. I came from Corinth, my most gracious
lord,—

Dro. E. And I with him.

Ant. E. Brought to this town by that most fa-
mous warrior,
Duke Menaphon, your most renowned uncle.

Adr. Which of you two did dine with me to-day?

Ant. S. I, gentle mistress.

Adr.   And are not you my husband?   370

Ant. E. No; I say nay to that.

Ant. S. And so do I; yet did she call me so:
And this fair gentlewoman, her sister here,
Did call me brother. [*To Luciana*] What I
told you then,
I hope I shall have leisure to make good;
If this be not a dream I see and hear.

Ang. That is the chain, sir, which you had of me.

Ant. S. I think it be, sir; I deny it not.

Ant. E. And you, sir, for this chain arrested me.

Ang. I think I did, sir; I deny it not.   381

Adr. I sent you money, sir, to be your bail,
By Dromio; but I think he brought it not.

Dro. E. No, none by me.

Ant. S. This purse of ducats I received from you,
    And Dromio my man did bring them me.
    I see we still did meet each other's man;
    And I was ta'en for him, and he for me;
    And thereupon these ERRORS are arose.

Ant. E. These ducats pawn I for my father here.

Duke. It shall not need; thy father hath his life.

Cour. Sir, I must have that diamond from you. 391

Ant. E. There, take it; and much thanks for my
    good cheer.

Abb. Renowned Duke, vouchsafe to take the pains
    To go with us into the abbey here,
    And hear at large discoursed all our fortunes:
    And all that are assembled in this place,
    That by this sympathized one day's error
    Have suffer'd wrong, go keep us company,
    And we shall make full satisfaction.
    Thirty-three years have I but gone in travail
    Of you, my sons; and till this present hour 401
    My heavy burthen ne'er delivered.
    The Duke, my husband, and my children both,

388. *"These* ERRORS *are arose,"* so the Folios; *are* has been variously changed by scholars into *all, rare,* but no change is necessary; as far as rhythm is concerned the Folio reading is certainly preferable.— I. G.

400. *"Thirty-three years";* this reading of the Folios has been changed to *twenty-five* by most editors, following Theobald, who calculates the age of the twins by putting together what Ægeon says in Act I. i. 125 and in line 320 of Act V. Capell suggested *twenty-three,* from Act. I. i. line 125 and line 133. On the other hand, the Duke states in line 326 of the present Act that he has been patron to Antipholus for "twenty years"; it looks as though Shakespeare changed his idea as to the age of the twins towards the end of the play, without troubling to make all his references fit in with one another.— I. G.

And you the calendars of their nativity,
Go to a gossips' feast, and go with me;
After so long grief, such nativity!

Duke. With all my heart, I'll gossip at this feast.
                    [*Exeunt all but Ant. S., Ant. E.,*
                         Dro. S., and Dro. E.

Dro. S. Master, shall I fetch your stuff from ship-
          board?

Ant. E. Dromio, what stuff of mine hast thou em-
          bark'd?

Dro. S. Your goods that lay at host, sir, in the
          Centaur.   410

Ant. S. He speaks to me. I am your master,
          Dromio:

Come, go with us; we'll look to that anon:
Embrace thy brother there; rejoice with him.
                    [*Exeunt Ant. S. and Ant. E.*

Dro. S. There is a fat friend at your master's
          house,

That kitchen'd me for you to-day at dinner:
She now shall be my sister, not my wife.

Dro. E. Methinks you are my glass, and not my
          brother:

I see by you I am a sweet-faced youth.

---

404. "*And you the calendars of their nativity*"; *i. e.,* the two
Dromios; *cp.* "Here comes the almanac of my true date," I. ii. 41.—
I. G.

406. "*After so long grief, such nativity*"; the laboring line har-
monizes well with the emotion of the speaker; the line is evidently
intended to be read as follows:—

          "*After | sō lōng | grīēf, süch | natĭv | ĭty.*"

There seems no reason for changing *nativity*, though Hammer's conjecture *felicity* has been accepted by most editors; Johnson proposed
festivity.—I. G.

Will you walk in to see their gossiping?

Dro. S. Not I, sir; you are my elder.   420

Dro. E. That's a question: how shall we try it?

Dro. S. We'll draw cuts for the senior: till then
    lead thou first.

Dro. E. Nay, then, thus:

    We came into the world like brother and
      brother;

    And now let's go hand in hand, not one before
      another.   [*Exeunt.*

GLOSSARY

By Israel Gollancz, M.A.

Advised, well informed of, deliberate concerning; V. i. 214.

Albeit, although; V. i. 217.

Amain, with might and main; I. i. 93.

Anatomy, skeleton; V. i. 238.

Angels; an angel was an English coin, worth about ten shillings; IV. iii. 43.

Apparently, obviously; IV. i. 78.

Armadoes, armadas; III. ii. 142.

A-row, in a row, one after another; V. i. 170.

Assured, affianced; III. ii. 147.

Attach, arrest; IV. i. 6.

Attaint, disgrace; III. ii. 16.

Austerely, seriously; IV. ii. 2.

Back-friend, an adversary; perhaps applied quibblingly to the sergeant, "because he comes from behind to arrest one"; IV. ii. 37.

Ballast, ballasted, loaded; III. ii. 143.

Band, bond (used equivocally); IV. ii. 49.

Beads, rosary; II. ii. 190.

Bear, carry off; V. i. 8.

Become, render becoming; III. ii. 11.

Belike, 'tis likely; IV. i. 25.

Bestow, employ, make use of; IV. i. 16.

Bestowed, stowed, deposited; I. ii. 78.

Bestrid; "b. thee," i. e. "defended thee when fallen"; V. i. 192.

Board, table; III. ii. 18.

Bought and sold, deluded and overreached by foul practices; III. i. 72.

By; "send me by some token"; a not uncommon Elizabethan idiom, meaning "give me some token whereby I may show that you have sent me"; IV. i. 56.

Caracks, galleons, large ships of burden; III. ii. 143.

Caract, carat; IV. i. 28.

Carcanet, necklace; III. i. 4.

Careful, full of care; V. i. 298.

Carriage, bearing; III. ii. 14.

Carved, made amorous gestures; II. ii. 120.

Case; "an action upon the case is a general action given for the redress of a wrong done any man without force, and not especially provided for by law"; IV. ii. 42.

Cates, dainties; III. i. 28.

Charged, gave in charge; III. i. 8.

Chargeful, expensive; IV. i. 29.

Children (trisyllabic); V. i. 360.

Choleric; the choleric man was advised "to abstain from all salt, scorched, dry meats, from mustard, and such like things as might aggravate his malignant humors"; II. ii. 63.

CIRCUMSTANCE, detail; V. i. 16.

CLAIM; "my heaven's claim," *i. e.* "all that I claim from heaven hereafter"; III. ii. 64.

CLEAN, entirely; I. i. 134.

COIL, ado; III. i. 48.

COLDLY, coolly; V. i. 272.

COMMON; "make a c. of," *i. e.* "use as a play-ground"; II. ii. 29.

COMPACT OF, wholly composed of; III. ii. 22.

COMPANION (used contemptuously), fellow; IV. iv. 64.

CONCEIT, conception; III. ii. 34; apprehension; IV. ii. 65.

CONFISCATE, confiscated; I. i. 21.

CONFOUNDS, destroys; I. ii. 38.

CONFUSION, ruin; II. ii. 182.

CONSORT, to keep company with; I. ii. 28.

COUNTERMANDS, stops one going through; IV. ii. 37.

COZENAGE, cheating; I. ii. 97.

CREDIT, credulity; III. ii. 22.

CURTAIL, having a docked tail; III. ii. 154.

CUSTOMERS (used contemptuously), visitors, guests; IV. iv. 63.

CUTS; papers cut of unequal lengths, of which the longest was usually the prize; hence, "to draw cuts"="to draw lots"; V. i. 422.

DANKISH, dampish; V. i. 247.

DEADLY, deathly; IV. iv. 96.

DEATH; "the death," *i. e.* "death by judicial sentence"; I. i. 147.

DEBTED, indebted; IV. i. 31.

DECIPHERS, distinguishes; V. i. 334.

DECLINE, incline; III. ii. 44.

DECLINING, inclining; III. ii. 140.

DEFEATURES, disfigurements; II. i. 98; V. i. 299.

DEFORMED, deforming; V. i. 298.

DEMEAN, conduct; IV. iii. 83.

DENIED (followed by a tautological negative); IV. ii. 7.

DESPITE OF; "in d. of mirth," *i. e.* "though I feel despiteful towards mirth"; III. i. 108.

DETAIN, withhold; II. i. 107.

DILATE, narrate; I. i. 123.

DISANNUL, annul; I. i. 145.

DISCHARGED, paid; IV. i. 32.

DISPENSE WITH, put up with; II. i. 103.

DISPOSE, disposal; I. i. 21.

DISPOSED, disposed of; I. ii. 73.

DISTAIN'D, sullied, disgraced; II. ii. 148.

DISTEMPERATURES, distempers; V. i. 82.

DISTRACT, distracted; IV. iii. 42.

DIVINER, sorceress; III. ii. 146.

DOWSABEL, a poetic name, used occasionally in Elizabethan writers generically for a beautiful lass (*douce et belle*); ironically applied by Dromio of Syracuse to the wench whose real name is Nell; IV. i. 110.

DRAWS DRY-FOOT, traces the scent of the game; "perhaps so called because, according to sportsmen, in water the scent is lost"; IV. ii. 39.

DRY, hard, severe; II. ii. 64.

DURANCE; v. "everlasting garment"; IV. iii. 28.

EARNEST, used quibblingly with reference to the sense of "earnest-money"; II. ii. 24.

ECSTASY, frenzy, madness; IV. iv. 54.

89

EVERLASTING GARMENT, alluding to "the buff jerkin" of the sergeant,—"a suit of durance" as it was called; IV. ii. 33.

EXCREMENT, outgrowth (applied to hair); II. ii. 79.

EXEMPT, separated; II. ii. 173.

FAIR, fairness, beauty; II. i. 98.

FAITH; "breast . . . of faith"; ("flint" has been adopted by some editors, but there is not sufficient reason for the change; by faith men resisted a witch's power); III. ii. 153.

FALL, let fall; II. ii. 127.

FALSING, (?) apt to be falsified; II. ii. 95.

FINE AND RECOVERY, a legal term, said to be "the strongest assurance known to English law"; II. ii. 75.

FINGER, "to put the f. in the eye," i. e. "to weep in a childish way"; II. ii. 206.

FLY PRIDE, "a proverbial phrase, by which Dromio rebukes the woman, whom he thinks a cheat, for accusing his master of cheating"; IV. iii. 85.

FOLDED, concealed; III. ii. 36.

FOND, doting; II. i. 116.

FONDLY, foolishly; IV. ii. 57.

FOOL-BEGG'D, foolishly begged or demanded; II. i. 41.

FORMAL, ordinary, rational; V. i. 105.

FORSWORE, "forswore to have," i. e. "swore that he did not have"; V. i. 11.

FORTH, "to find f." i. e. "to find out"; I. ii. 37; away from home; II. ii. 212.

FOR WHY, because; III. ii. 105.

FRAUGHTAGE, freight; IV. i. 87.

GENIUS, attendant spirit; V. i. 332.

GET WITHIN, close with, grapple with; V. i. 34.

GILLIAN = Juliana; III. i. 31.

GINN = Jenny; III. i. 31.

GOOD NOW = good fellow now (others explain the phrase as equivalent to "well now"); IV. iv. 22.

GOSSIP, make merry; V. i. 407.

GOSSIPING, merry-making (with a probable reference to original sense, a sponsors' feast); V. i. 419.

GOSSIPS, sponsors; V. i. 405.

GRAIN, "in grain," i. e. "in-grained, deeply dyed"; III. ii. 108.

GRAINED, furrowed (like the grain of wood); V. i. 311.

GROWING, accruing; IV. i. 8.

GUILDERS, Dutch coins of the value of about two shillings; used in a general sense for "money"; I. i. 8.

HARLOTS, lewd fellows; V. i. 205.

HATCH, half-door, wicket; III. i. 33.

HEALTHFUL, full of safety; I. i. 115.

HEART'S METEORS, "alluding to those meteors in the sky (the aurora borealis) which have the appearance of lines of armies meeting in the shock"; IV. ii. 6.

HEIR (with a play upon hair, cf. Preface); III. ii. 127.

HELL, used quibblingly; the cant term for an obscure dungeon; IV. ii. 40.

HELPLESS, unavailing; II. i. 39.

HIS, its; II. i. 110.

HIT OF, hit on, guess; III. ii. 30.

HOLP, helped; IV. i. 22.

HORN-MAD, "mad like a wicked bull; generally used with a reference to cuckoldry"; II. i. 58.

HOST, "lay at h. in," *i. e.* "were put up at"; V. i. 410.

HOST, lodge; I. ii. 9.

HOY, a small vessel, a kind of sloop; IV. iii. 42.

IMPEACH, impeachment; V. i. 269.

IMPORTANT, importunate; V. i. 138.

INSTANCE, indication; I. i. 65.

INTESTINE, internal; I. i. 11.

JEST UPON, trifle with; II. ii. 28.

JUDGMENT, "before the J." there is perhaps a quibbling allusion in the phrase to what is called *mesne-process;* IV. ii. 40.

KITCHEN'D, entertained in the kitchen; V. i. 415.

LAPLAND; Shakespeare's sole reference to Lapland sorcerers (*cp.* Milton's "Lapland witches"); IV. iii. 11.

LASH'D, scourged (with perhaps a reference to "lashed" in the sense of "fastened, bound"); II. i. 15.

LETS, hinders; II. i. 105.

LIBERTIES, libertinisms, "l. of sin," *i. e.* "licensed offenders"; I. ii. 102.

LIGHT, wanton (used equivocally); IV. iii. 52.

LIMBO, a cant term for "prison," properly, "hell," or "the borders of hell"); IV. ii. 32.

LOVE-SPRINGS, shoots of love; III. ii. 3.

MACE, a sergeant's club; IV. iii. 29.

MADE, barred; III. i. 93.

MAKING, outward form; IV. ii. 22.

MALT-HORSE, a dull, heavy horse, like a brewer's, used contemptuously; III. i. 32.

MATED, used quibblingly in the sense of "confounded," and "given as a mate"; III. ii. 54.

MERMAID, siren; III. ii. 45.

MICKLE, much; III. i. 45.

MINION, favorite (used contemptuously), darling; IV. iv. 66; *pl.* II. i. 87.

MOME, buffoon; III. i. 32.

MOOD, anger; II. ii. 172.

MORRIS-PIKE, a Moorish pike; IV. iii. 29.

MORTAL, deadly; I. i. 11.

MOTIONS, proposals; I. i. 60.

MOVES, appeals to; II. ii. 183.

NATURE, natural affection; I. i. 35.

NEW-APPARELLED (*vide* Notes); IV. iii. 14.

NICKS, "n. him like a fool," alluding to the old custom of shaving, nicking, or notching the head of a professional buffoon; V. i. 175.

O'ER-RAUGHT, overcalled, cheated; I. ii. 96.

OF, out of, from; I. i. 131; "wreck of sea" (so first Folio, the rest "at sea") = off, out at sea; V. i. 49.

ON, "on night," *i. e.* "a-night"; V. i. 210.

ONCE THIS; "so much is certain"; III. i. 89.

ORDER, measures; V. i. 146.

OTHER, "no other cause," *i. e.*

"no cause to be otherwise"; II. i. 33.

Owe, own; III. i. 42.

Pack'd, leagued; V. i. 219.

Parcel, part; V. i. 106.

Part, depart; III. i. 67.

Partial, "I am not p. to infringe," *i. e.* "I am not so inclined in your behalf as to infringe"; I. i. 4.

Passage, the going to and fro of people; III. i. 99.

Patch, fool, jester; III. i. 32.

Peasant, servant; V. i. 231.

Peevish, foolish; IV. i. 93.

Penitent, doing penance; I. ii. 52.

Perdie, *par dieu!* IV. iv. 77

Perforce, by force; IV. iii. 99.

Peruse, survey; I. ii. 13.

Plainings, wailings; I. i. 73.

Please, pay; IV. iv. 52.

Porpentine, Porcupine (the only form of the word used by Shakespeare); III. i. 116.

Post, post-haste; I. ii. 63.

Post, used quibblingly; an allusion to keeping the score by chalk or notches on a post; I. ii. 64.

Presently, immediately; III. ii. 156.

Quit, remit; I. i. 23.

Rag, shred, particle; IV. iv. 92.

Rest; "sets up his rest"; Dromio plays on "rest," "arrest," and a metaphor, "setting up his rest," taken from gaming, and meaning "staking his all" upon an event; IV. iii. 28.

Reverted, turned back; III. ii. 126.

Road, harbor; III. ii. 156.

Round, used quibblingly in the sense of (1) "spherical," and (2) "plain-spoken"; II. i. 82.

Runs counter, follows the scent backward instead of forward; with a play perhaps upon "Counter," the name of two London prisons; IV. ii. 39.

Sconce, a helmet (originally a small fort, bulwark), applied also to the head itself; I. ii. 79; II. ii. 34; II. ii. 37.

Scorch, excoriate; V. i. 183.

Season, opportunity; "to s."= "at the opportune time"; IV. ii. 58.

Semblance (trisyllabic); V. i. 358.

Sensible (used equivocally in ordinary sense and in sense of "sensitive"); IV. iv. 28.

Sere, dry, withered; IV. ii. 19.

Shapeless, unshapely; IV. ii. 20.

Shrive, call to confession; II. ii. 210.

Sinking-ripe, ripe for sinking, ready to sink; I. i. 78.

Sir-reverence, a corruption of "save-reverence" (contracted into "sa'reverence") a translation of Lat. *salvâ reverentiâ; save-reverence* or *save your reverence* was considered "a sufficient apology for anything indecorous"; III. ii. 93.

Sob (first folio reads "fob," *i. e.* sob, probably an error for "fob," which was used by Elizabethan writers in the sense of a slight blow); IV. iii. 25.

Soon, nearly; "s. at five o'clock," *i. e.* "about five o'clock"; I. ii. 26.

Soothe, humor; IV. iv. 85.

Sorry, pitiable, sad; V. i. 121.

Sot, dolt; II. ii. 196.

Sour (dissyllabic; "sower" in the Folios); V. i. 45.

Spite, vexation; IV. ii. 8.

Spoon-meat (used equivocally, to introduce allusion to the proverb, "he must have a long spoon that must eat with the devil"; IV. iii. 65.

Stale, "second woman," the one to fall back on if another is not to be had; II. i. 101.

Stands upon, concerns; IV. i. 68.

Stigmatical, marked or stigmatized with deformity; IV. ii. 22.

Stomach, appetite; I. ii. 49.

Stray'd, caused to stray; V. i. 51.

Strong; "s. escape," i. e. "escape effected by *strength,* or violence"; V. i. 148.

Strumpeted, made a strumpet of; II. ii. 146.

Stuff, baggage; IV. iv. 156.

Supposed, conjectured; III. i. 101.

Suspect, suspicion; III. i. 87.

Sympathized, mutually suffered; V. i. 397.

Take; "t. a house," i. e. "take sanctuary in a house"; V. i. 36.

Tartar, Tartarian; it is noteworthy that Tartarian was a cant term for "thief"; IV. ii. 32.

Tilting, v. Heart's Meteors.

Timely, speedy; I. i. 139.

Tiring, attiring; II. ii. 99.

To, of; III. ii. 170.

Took on him as, pretended to be; V. i. 242.

Train, entice; III. ii. 45.

Turn i' the wheel; "there is comprehended, under the curs of the coarsest kind, a certain dog in kitchen service excellent; for when any meat is to be roasted, they go into a wheel, which they turning round about with the weight of their bodies, so diligently look to their business, that no drudge nor scullion can do the feat more cunningly" (Topsell, *History of Four-footed beasts,* 1607); III. ii. 153.

Understand (used quibblingly with a play upon "understand" ="stand under"); II. i. 49.

Ungalled, unblemished; III. i. 102.

Unhappy, mischievous; IV. iv. 130.

Untuned, discordant; V. i. 310.

Vain, light of tongue; III. ii. 27.

Villain (used good-humoredly); I. ii. 19.

Vulgar, public; III. i. 100.

Waftage, passage; IV. i. 95.

Wafts, beckons; II. ii. 111.

Week; perhaps with a play upon "wick" (pronounced like "week"); III. ii. 103.

Well-advised, acting with due deliberation, in right mind; II. ii. 215.

When? Can you tell? "a proverbial inquiry indicating the improbability that the person addressed will get what he asks"; III. i. 52.

When as, whenas, i. e. when; IV. iv. 143.

Whether (monosyllabic, printed "whe'r" in the Folios); IV. i. 60.

Wink, to shut the eyes; III. ii. 58.

Wont, is wont (to bear); IV. iv. 40.

STUDY QUESTIONS

By Anne Throop Craig

GENERAL

1. What is the earliest reference to this play?

2. What points of external evidence are helpful in fixing the time of this play's writing?

3. From what is the main plot derived?

4. Indicate the leading points of difference between the Latin farce and this play?

5. What characteristic Shakespearean element does the Ægeon episode introduce?

6. From what point of view and in what way may the *Comedy of Errors* be regarded as a triumph of the New Romantic Drama over its opponents?

7. What are the evidences in the play itself that it is one of the poet's earliest performances?

8. What makes this play more diverting than the *Menæchmi* of Plautus?

9. In what more natural way than by a prologue does Shakespeare sketch the foundation story of the play?

10. Distinguish a farce from a comedy.

11. Is development of character to be expected in such a play as this? Give reasons.

12. What does Coleridge have to say of this farce?

13. What is the effect of Shakespeare's use of seriously impending tragic events in his early comedies? Cite and compare instances.

14. In what way are Luciana's passages distinctive?

15. How does Pinch accord with the setting of the play?

16. Why is Adriana a notable instance of the Poet's

insight into fundamental character? Has Adriana's discontent its modern counterpart?

17. What must always enter into the work of a true poet to prevent its being superficial? What element in this play keeps it from the pure superficiality of farce? If such an element gives it more weight in some respects, does overweigh it, artistically, considered as pure farce?

18. What were probably the elements of nature and purpose that made Shakespeare write no other farce than this?

ACT I

19. Why was Ægeon to be beheaded?

20. What story did he tell?

21. What chance for his life did the Duke give him?

22. What does Antipholus of Syracuse send his Dromio to do?

23. Between whom is the first mistaken encounter in the play?

24. What message does Dromio of Ephesus deliver to Antipholus of Syracuse?

25. What does Dromio of Ephesus mean in line 64?

26. How does Antipholus of Syracuse receive the mistaken message? How does he serve Dromio of Ephesus for it?

ACT II

27. Are Adriana and Luciana distinctively characterized at their introduction?

28. How does Dromio of Ephesus describe his encounter with Antipholus of Syracuse to Adriana? How does she receive it?

29. What is Adriana's mood, and its cause?

30. Between which Dromio and which Antipholus is the encounter in scene ii? Describe it.

31. Into what state of mind does the tangle throw Antipholus of Syracuse and his Dromio, in scene ii after the entrance of Adriana and Luciana?

ACT III

32. What is the first complication involving all tl doubles at once?　Describe it.

33. What does Balthasar advise?　Why does not A₁ tipholus of Ephesus take his advice?

34. Where does Antipholus of Ephesus decide to g when he cannot get into his own house?

35. Does Adriana appear to give Antipholus of Ephes₁ some cause for occasionally going elsewhere for entertai₁ ment?

36. In what mood does Antipholus of Ephesus decide ₁ take the gift intended for his wife, to the courtesan i₁ stead?　What is the gift?

37. What impression does Luciana make on Antiphol₁ of Syracuse?

38. How does she receive his protestations?

39. What does Dromio of Syracuse recount of his u₁ welcome adventure at Adriana's house?

40. Where does the incident of the gift to the Courtes₁ begin to take on importance in the plot?

ACT IV

41. Describe the further developments centering abo₁ the incident of the chain, in scene i.　How do they invol' Antipholus of Ephesus and his Dromio?

42. What is the comic element in Dromio of Syracu₁ calling the fat cook "Dowsabel" in line 110, scene i From what is the name derived?

43. What errand is Dromio of Ephesus sent upon, ₁ Adriana, in scene ii?

44. What does Antipholus of Syracuse relate of his a₁ ventures in Ephesus, in scene iii?

45. With what performance does Dromio of Syracu₁ surprise his own master in this scene?

46. What person unknown to him accosts Antipholus ₁ Syracuse as an acquaintance in scene iii?　In connectio₁

vith this incident how does his wearing the chain Angelo
ias given him, further tangle the plot?

47. What does the Courtesan conclude as to the state of
nind of Antipholus?   What does she decide to do about
t?

48. What mistaken encounter is described in scene iv?
Vhat comes of it?

49. Describe the diagnosis Dr. Pinch makes of the con-
lition of Antipholus.   What does it satirize?

50. What is the conclusion of all with regard to the con-
lition of Antipholus of Ephesus and his Dromio?   What
s done with them accordingly?

51. What does the Courtesan tell of her ring?

52. What surprise immediately follows for the three
women, as they stand conversing?

53. What does Antipholus of Syracuse decide he wishes
to do as quickly as possible at the ending of this act?

ACT V

54. What next *contretemps* awaits Antipholus of Syracuse in scene i?   What is its outcome?

55. How does Adriana prevent the fight between Antipholus of Syracuse and the Second Merchant?

56. What refuge do Antipholus of Syracuse and his
Dromio take?

57. What does the Abbess do?

58. Is the Abbess's rebuke of Adriana justified?   How
does Adriana receive it?   What is the dramatic use of the
Abbess's rebuke?

59. Describe the final resolution of the play.   Contrast
its elements with the usual ones of farce.

60. Characterize the management of the resolution, as
to disposition of groupings and interaction of motives
leading to it.   Is it balanced, smooth?—are the threads
well and convincingly collected?   Analyze in detail.

VI—7